Accl
Sunda

MW01286987

"My friend Greg Asimakoupoulos is a respected poet from the District I represent in Washington State. His inspirational verse has encouraged me during my years on Capitol Hill. In fact, I have a framed poem by Pastor Greg that hangs in my office in Washington, D.C."

– The Honorable Dave Reichert
U.S. Congressman 8th District

"Greg Asimakoupoulos has a unique insight for every occasion. No one I know captures the moment better! I find myself both quoting him and being inspired by him through my own fresh insights. You too will find him so helpful."

– Dr. John A. Huffman, Jr., Senior Pastor
St. Andrews Presbyterian Church, Newport Beach, CA

"You don't have to be an avid reader of poetry to enjoy and benefit from Greg Asimakoupoulos' new book of poems. It contains many prayer prompts for small groups, and illustrations for teaching or communication pieces."

– Phil Miglioratti, Director
the National Pastors' Prayer Network

"Pastor Greg is our mission's unofficial poet laureate. He captures the emotions of needing, getting and giving a wheelchair that melts the hearts of our supporters. His poetic gift is making this world a better place."

– Dr. Don Schoendorfer, President and Founder
Free Wheelchair Mission

"It's Saturday night - you're the shepherd of the flock and your sermon is perfect--almost! Well, fear not - Pastor/Poet Greg has creatively prepared the icing on the cake for you and your congregation to enjoy."

– Peggie C. Bohanon, editor of peggiesplace.com

"Poetry is so much more than cadence and rhyme. It is the elegant (and sometimes playful) expression of ideas that compels us to stop and think, to wonder and reflect. Greg Asimakoupoulos' poetry gives voice to what we have felt and known, but could not articulate. "

> – Rev. Jim Lyon, national radio host of ViewPoint

"Like the shifting shades and silhouettes of clouds that parade across God's celestial palette, my friend Greg's poetic expressions conform to the message His Creator has placed on his heart at the moment."

> – George Toles, President, The Toles Company

"Sunday Rhymes & Reasons is an uplifting collection sure to inspire, delight, and humor. Written from the perspective of a pastor, it captures our most precious church memories while addressing the issues of our day. A stirring book that is sure to strengthen your faith!"

> – Shelly Esser, Editor, Just Between Us Magazine

"Sunday Rhymes and Reasons links faith and life together in a heartfelt and meaningful way. Greg uses his special gift of poetry to touch my emotions in ways no other poet does. "

> – Al Lopus, President, Best Christian Workplaces Institute

"This book will introduce you to a unique ministry -- one that combines rhyme and reason in the service of faith. I wouldn't be surprised if it inspires the Almighty to re-write the Ten Commandments in rhyming couplets. "

> – Dave Ross, CBS radio network commentator

SUNDAY RHYMES & REASONS

*Inspirational poems for pastors,
leaders and other imperfect saints*

SUNDAY RHYMES& REASONS

Inspirational poems for pastors,
leaders and other imperfect saints

by Greg Asimakoupoulos

Partial Observer Books
Lynchburg, Virginia

Published June 2009

Many of the poems contained within Sunday Rhymes and
Reasons originally appeared on The Partial Observer at
partialobserver.com.

ISBN 1494849860
ISBN-13 978-1494849863

Cover illustration and book design by Mark D. Johnson

Partial Observer Books
www.partialobserver.com

This volume is dedicated to my late father,
The Reverend Edwin Asimakoupoulos,
(March 14, 1926 – November 4, 2008)
whose example taught me the power of poetry in a
sermon. His brave battle with prostate cancer
provided me with many reasons for Sunday rhymes.

CONTENTS

FOREWORD

I love to read poetry. I enjoy writing it even more. Hardly a day goes by I don't scribble a stanza or two. There is just something about poems that defies explanation. Like a housecat, they have a way of curling up on the couch of our culture and making themselves at home without fanfare.

Although poetry doesn't claim the popularity that it once did, I am amazed at how often rhyming sentiments are shared at weddings, graduation parties, anniversaries and funerals. It seems that such heart-moments call for language that dances with meter and metaphors. Occasions like these prove that linear language is not sufficient to carry the day.

Poetry is multidimensional. It can paint a picture, provide a vocabulary for the indescribable and penetrate the emotions. Sometime back I reflected on the power of poetic expression in a piece I titled "A Cultural Necessity."

There are times you need a poem
to express the pain inside.
Words fall short as feelings lengthen
and in sorrow thoughts can lie.

Poets have a way of sifting
through the rubble of our grief.
In their lyrical expressions,
mourners often find relief.

When they sense God's holy presence
and are silenced by His grace,
they're amazed how poets' brushes
can portray His unseen face.

And when joy exceeds description
at a wedding or a birth,
there is nothing like a poem
to convey life's deepest mirth.

Ever notice just how often
someone quotes some poetry?
In an ocean of emotion
rhyming verses calm the sea.

So when asked if I'm a poet,
I don't wince and hang my head.
I can't think of a vocation
that I'd rather claim instead.

When I was in seminary, I was reminded of the historic place poetry claimed in the American pulpit. For countless decades preachers relied on poetry as a means of punctuating a point in their sermon. My homiletics professor humorously observed that the typical sermon included an introduction, three points and a poem.

While poems aren't as common in sermons (in newspapers or even the classroom) as they once were, poetry continues to be a literary means of providing the naked truth with appropriate clothing. Through poetry, emotions and ideas are incarnated. In a poem, descriptive words become flesh and "dwell among us."

Sunday Rhymes and Reasons is a collection of poetry that celebrates faith, welcomes doubt, acknowledges the predictable passages of life and points to God. As the subtitle suggests, it is intended for pastors, leaders and other imperfect saints. I hope this book of "uncommon prayer" and poetic commentary on culture will provide a personal resource for spiritual reflection, meditation and even a few laughs.

By my own admission, my poetry is not esoteric or highbrow. It would not likely win awards among poetry societies. While you will find some blank verse in the pages that follow, most of my poetry has a predictable meter and traditional rhyme. That is intentional. My desire is to communicate simply and memorably rather than to string together abstract phrases that require a high degree of concentration to achieve understanding.

Feel free to pass along poems that address a particular challenge currently faced by a family member or friend. Pastors and Sunday school teachers might very well find resources in this little volume that can be shared from a pulpit or a lectern.

In addition to poems that relate to Sundays (themes about worship, prayer, liturgy and the like), there are also poems that speak to Week Days or "Weak Days" (when we find ourselves dwarfed by everyday challenges), Special Days (such as baptisms, weddings, funerals, etc.), Holidays (like New Years, Memorial Day, Thanksgiving, etc.), Holy Days (specifically Advent, Christmas, Good Friday and Easter), and Bible Days (poetic paraphrases of well-known personalities or events in Scripture).

Since 2003 I have written a weekly poetry column for partialobserver.com , a website that offers a variety of commentaries on politics, popular culture, religion and the arts. My weekly blog on this site is called *Rhymes and Reasons*.

Many of the poems in this volume are taken from The Partial Observer website. Most, however, have never been published. It is my hope that you will enjoy *Sunday Rhymes and Reasons* as much as I enjoyed writing it.

God's Artists

Poets are God's artists.
With pen in hand
they sketch the world
with ink and words and metaphors.
They do what they adore.
In the process
they draw a door to truth
for those who seek to knock.
Poets, you see, are finders
who are not content to keep
their treasures to themselves.
They must express
what they confess to see.
It's a passion that burns within them.
Awake to life (their hearts afire),
poets pray on paper.
They are keepers of the flame
that blazes in the soul of humankind.

Greg Asimakoupoulos
May 2009

SUNDAYS

Waiting for Worship

As I sit in silence
for the service to begin,
I wonder how the living Lord
will speak to me again.

Will it be the songs we sing
or in the pastor's prayer?
It just might be the sermon
or a need someone will share.

Maybe God will touch my heart
through laughter or a sigh.
Perhaps through some distraction
like a newborn's hungry cry.

Whatever means God uses
as He bends my ear His way,
I will listen with expectancy
for there's something He will say.

The Many Faces of Worship

Our worship's more than singing.
We worship when we pray.
We worship when the preacher speaks
and then when we obey.

We worship when, in silence,
we assume a humble stance.
We worship when we raise our arms
or when we start to dance.

It's showing God we love Him
or whispering His name.
It's what we do with grateful hearts.
To God it's all the same.

Worship Without End

I don't have to wait for Sunday
to sing praises or to pray.
I can worship God regardless
of the hour or the day.

I don't need a stone cathedral;
I don't need a padded pew.
And though stained windows are quite nice,
most any pane will do.

I enjoy the choir's anthem
and I love the preacher's talk.
But I can sense God's presence
in my car or on a walk.

While it's true I need a Sabbath
and the fellowship of friends,
I'm not limited to Sundays.
It's called worship without end.

Come to Jesus

Come to Jesus
broken, bleeding,
lonely, sorrow-filled.
Come to Jesus,
let Him love you.
Let your restless soul be stilled.

Come to Jesus,
in your struggle
with addictions,
straight or gay.
Come to Jesus,
saint or sinner.
Let Him love your doubts away.

Come to Jesus,
worn and weary,
those whose joy
has been sucked dry.
Come to Jesus
with your passions
and your shattered dreams
and whys.

In My Heart There Rings a Memory

Be Still My Soul, I tell myself,
so stress won't undermine my health.
There's so much cause for worry
in a world that's marked by pain.

And then I think of gospel hymns
whose lyrics take me back again
to times we lingered at the church
to lift up Jesus' name.

Remember when *How Great Thou Art*
would be the song with which we'd start
an old-time singspiration
after church on Sunday nights?

And then we'd sing *At Calvary,*
Down at the Cross and *I Believe.*
We'd close our eyes and harmonize
around that old upright.

I never will forget those days
when *At the Cross* and *Jesus Saves*
transported me to *Gloryland*
somewhere beyond the blue.

We'd Stand Amazed In Times Like These
and then we'd get down on our knees
to *Have a Little Talk with Jesus*
till at last we'd all prayed through.

I miss *The Wonder of It All*
when *Face to Face* we'd hear Christ call.
In soft and tender words of love,
he'd speak *Whispering Hope.*

Those after-meetings filled with song
are precious times for which I long.
Perhaps if we embraced old ways,
we'd find new ways to cope.

Confessions of a Praise-Song Critic

I grew up singing from a book.
I loved those gospel hymns.
Like *What a Friend* and *Jesus Saves*
and *Marching to Zion.*

With Dad and Mother by my side,
we'd sing in harmony.
The lyrics to *Amazing Grace*
would always comfort me.

That hymnal came to represent
sweet memories of past days.
Its pages, like old photographs,
were more than songs of praise.

I don't recall just when it was
it all began to change.
I just remember what we sang
was fast and loud and strange.

I didn't know these choruses.
I missed the good old songs.

And though the church began to grow,
I doubted I belonged.
But then one day I looked around
and saw my daughter's face.
I wept to see her worshiping;
eyes closed and hands upraised.

That Sunday changed my attitude.
I started to rejoice.
I asked the Lord to help me sing
what I'd considered noise.

Through *Awesome God* and *Famous One*,
He changed my heart, I guess.
I now can worship joyfully.
But may I still confess?

I still would rather hold a book
and voice hymns I recall
than stand for almost half an hour
while singing off the wall.

** Although I have a deep appreciation for the great hymns of
the Church, I also appreciate the current trends in worship
music. I wrote this poem to provide my mom and dad (and
their generation) a means of verbalizing their struggle with
change in the Church.*

I Am Your Hymnal

Hold me with your hands.
Touch me with your eyes.
I think you'll be surprised.
My pages will soften the hardships you face.
I'm a gift of God's grace
that will set your faith to singing.
I'm bound to be enjoyed for years to come.
Yet, for years congregations have debated
(and at times berated each other)
over whether I still belong in church.
But if they'd search me, they would find
that I am not sectarian,
or contrarian to what true Christians seek.
The weak and those stronger,
the young and those older,
the new believer and the more mature
find their story in my pages.
And what is more,
I'm a link to the ages of those who lived before.
I'm an encyclopedia of Christian experience.
I'm a concordance of confession.
I'm a primer of praise.
I'm a diary of doctrinal truth.
I'm a one-volume library of devotion.
Handle me with care.
Handle me with prayer.
Handle me often.

Sunday Mourning at the Church of St. Relevancy.

Grieving the death of two liturgical friends.

Has anyone seen Gloria?
She's missing from my church.
Miss Patri taught me praise for God.
Please help me in my search.

"Doc" Sology is also gone.
I long to see him back.
I leaned on him when I was young.
He kept my praise on track.

But something changed. The songs got fast.
The Lord's Prayer went away.
Responsive readings from my past
were loudly drummed away.

My Sunday mornings aren't the same
since Gloria and "Doc"
were labeled too traditional
and forced to take a walk.

It's mourning time here in my pew.
Can you relate to me?
I have a hunch my friends have died
the death of liturgy.

The Sounds of Sunday

A hymn of praise.
A worship song.
A message from God's Word.
These clothe my anxious mind with peace
when life seems so absurd.
I close my eyes,
unlock my heart
and listen with my soul.
And through the lyrics of God's love,
my chaos is controlled.

These Sunday sounds
(like therapy)
drown out my restless fear.
Enveloped in the truth of God,
I know that He is near.

In Praise of Sundays

A day of rest? Hardly!
A day unlike all others
has become a day just like the rest,
as our culture tests
what "Sabbath" really means.

Trips back to the office.
Shopping at the mall.
Little League and soccer
on the green.
Homework on the table.
Projects in the yard.
E-notes to answer on the screen.

Still and yet, you can bet
some things will stay the same.
After all, it's Sunday
and that means…

Prayer time at the altar.
Communion at the rail.
Preachers dressed in robes
or coats and ties.
Sunday meals at Grandma's.
Strolls down country lanes.
Napping in a hammock
'neath blue skies.

With Praise for Hymns

There is nothing like a timeless hymn
that tunes my heart to praise.
There's *What a Friend* and *At the Cross*
and then there's *Jesus Saves*.

Those thoughtful words wash over me
and soothe my restless mind.
When *At the Cross, Just as I Am,*
My Savior's Love I find.

Hymns link me to a heritage
that stretches back in time
to others who (amazed by grace)
sang doctrine made to rhyme.

I do enjoy the worship songs
that cause me to look in.
But when it comes to looking up,
there's nothing like a hymn.

With Praise for Small Groups

A community of learners
with the Bible as our text,
we've discovered how the Scriptures
can bring comfort when we're vexed.
We've attested to the power
that is found when two or three
gather in the name of Jesus,
poised to learn expectantly.
We're committed to our small group.
We make time to come prepared.
And when we admit our struggles,
there is healing when we've shared.

So Blessed Are We

So long ago God whispered in a garden,
"It is not good for us to be alone."
We need companionship and affirmation.
Life can be hard, our hearts a heavy stone.
We long to be surrounded with compassion,
encouraged in the values that we own.

So steep, so difficult the trail we're climbing.
At times we wonder if we can go on.
We slip and fall. At times we're even bleeding.
Our journey can seem tortuous and long.
But when we walk in step with one another,
the darkest night becomes a hopeful dawn.

So let us be transparent with each other,
confessing things we hope for, fear and need.
Without the insight that a friend can offer,
we're often blind to ego, lust and greed.
Temptation's hold on us is strangely weakened,
when linked in prayer we boldly intercede.

So blessed are we to be joined to each other
on this adventure that we share as one.
The curse of loneliness has now been broken.
The joy of Heaven seems to have begun.
What God intended for His chosen offspring,
we know firsthand through friendship with His Son.

(tune: Finlandia)

Let's Hear it For Home Fellowships

It's a place for seeking wisdom
as we study to be wise,
as we page through God's instruction
that exposes culture's lies.

It's a place where we are molded
by what God defines as true
when it comes to wealth and family
and the worth of what we do.

It's a place we learn together
as we worship, pray and share
in a fellowship of friendship
that is really very rare.

It's a place that God has given
where His presence is made known
as we read His Book and ponder
how (by grace) our faith has grown.

Come Share This Meal

"Come share this meal," hear Jesus say.
A feast awaits this holy day.
With hunger pangs for righteousness,
approach Him now. Be filled and blessed.

The Savior's body is the bread,
the very one which for you bled.
Be nourished by His suffering,
as in your hearts you crown Him King.

Come as you are. You have a place
to drink His cup of boundless grace.
Your thirsty soul will be refreshed
as you draw near, your sins confessed.

Since all is ready don't delay.
Come share His feast this holy day.
With confidence confess your need,
as you by faith on Jesus feed.

Lord of All Nations

Lord of all nations, we are Your children.
Fearing the headlines, weary of war.
Gathered for worship, we seek You, Father,
trusting Your purpose for what's in store.

Lord, we are anxious. Help us to trust You.
Terror runs rampant throughout our land.
Fear dogs our footsteps. Worry soon follows.
When our faith buckles, help us to stand.

Lord, for the grieving, we plead Your comfort.
Mend broken hearts and minimize pain.
Marshal Your angels to lonely families.
Give them the means to call on Your name.

Lord, though our world is reeling around us,
we long for peace found only in You.
Grant us the grace to claim what You've promised.
Fill us with hope when reasons seem few.

(tune: Morning Has Broken)

Onward, Christian Shoulders

Onward, Christian shoulders.
Let the grieving cry.
They need you to lean on
when their loved ones die.
Shoulders are essential.
They are needed joints.
When someone is hurting,
they to Heaven point.

Onward, Christian shoulders.
Serve for Jesus' sake.
He is counting on you
when the heartsick ache.

Onward, Christian shoulders.
Let the burdened near.
Those weighed down by troubles.
Those consumed by fear.

Shoulders can be shelters
when we feel exposed.
They can bear the brunt of hardship,
bracing from life's woes

Onward, Christian shoulders.
Serve for Jesus' sake.
He is counting on you
when the wounded break.

(tune: Onward, Christian Soldiers)

A Sunday School Teacher's Prayer

O God, they sit before me week after week.
Those who want to learn and those who won't.
Those who trust me
and those who find it difficult to trust anyone.
How difficult my task, dear Lord.
Their trek toward truth is an awesome climb;
too dangerous and slippery to be traveled
without a guide.
I am willing, but I am only one.
Renew my weary spirit, Father.
Fill my mind with imaginative ways
of communicating concepts
these kids must learn in order to make it in the world.
Give me eyes to see what these young lives
may one day yet become.
And lest I cash in my chips of chalk in utter frustration,
please pass the patience.
They called Your Son The Teacher.
May His example energize me who shares His name
so that I may continue to cherish the children,

to view each student as one created in your image,
to lift up the downcast, to go the extra mile,
to lead by serving and love by listening,
to be satisfied with my best
and to trust you with the rest,
to grasp your values that never change
and to value your grasp of me in all that I attempt to do
for Jesus' sake. Amen.

Memories of My First Pastor

When I contemplate the people
God has used to touch my life,
I'm reminded of a gray-haired man
and his sweet, quiet wife.

Each Sunday he would stand to pray
and then begin to preach.
And though he wasn't eloquent,
I loved his halting speech.

He opened up the Bible
as he made those stories live.
I still can smell the loaves and fish
that boy was prone to give.

He'd shake hands with the grown-ups
after church when they would go.
And he would call us kids by name
and say "You're great, you know!"

SUNDAYS

Some nights he'd show up at our house
for coffee and to talk.
Or sometimes he would phone to share
a need within the flock.

Though not a theologian
with a long list of degrees,
my pastor grew in wisdom
as he spent time on his knees.

He could comfort folks at funerals
and at weddings he would cry.
When he counseled those in trouble,
he would listen, nod and sigh.

I learned from that dear man of God
that faith is clearly caught
when those who see the truth lived out
can trust what they are taught.

As I look back my heart is filled
with gratitude and joy
for one who led our little church
when I was just a boy.

That godly man and his dear wife
have long since passed away.
But since they led me to the Lord,
I'll see them both some day.

This poem is not autobiographical. My dad was my first pastor. I wrote this to reflect the experience of those who had a shepherd like the one described above.

A Prayer for My Pastor

Although it's blessed, his life is stressed.
His fuel gauge points to "E."
He's running out of energy
to do Your ministry.

The church's strife (just ask his wife)
has pinned him to the mat.
It seems the hurt from those he serves
is pain he must combat.

When members die, it makes him cry.
They are like family.
When they divorce, he's tied in knots.
He can't just let it be.

When critics snipe or deacons gripe,
his world's a living hell.
And when the offerings come up short,
he doesn't sleep real well.

So give him rest and curb the pests
that plague him every day.
Remind him that he's dearly loved.
In Jesus' name I pray. Amen.

The Shepherd of the Flock

My pastor's work is never done.
He's sermons to prepare.
And calls to make
and folks to see in dire need of care.

SUNDAYS

He spends time with the leadership
to shape the church's goals.
But he is just as comfortable
with ex-cons on parole.

He's at the bedside of the sick.
He's at his daughter's game.
He eulogizes those who've died.
He knows his flock by name.

He comforts widows in their grief.
He counsels single dads.
He hangs with kids to understand
their pressures, dreams and fads.

He mentors men who've lost their jobs.
He marries grooms and brides.
For those confused who need to talk,
in him they can confide.

He calms the staff when they are stressed.
He prays at Rotary.
He seeks out those he knows are new
in his community.

And yet in spite of all he does,
you won't hear him complain.
He's energized by all the ways
he serves in Jesus' name.

Benediction

As we go into the crossroads
of our hurried, harried lives,
there to meet a world God chooses
to release from fear and strife,
help us, Lord, to be Your body.
Fill us with Your life and power.
Animate us with Your Spirit.
Give us courage for this hour.

** I wrote this benediction in 1984 for Crossroads Covenant
Church in Concord, California, where I served for eleven years.
It can be sung to the tune of "Let All Mortal Flesh Keep
Silence" if you repeat the final phrasing of the melody to
accommodate the last two lines of the lyrics.*

WEEKDAYS
(or Weak Days)

A Daily Choice

When you're tempted
to doubt Him, don't do it.
Determine you'll trust God instead.
Don't feast on your fears
and your worries.
They only feed nightmares in bed.

Don't nibble your nails
all befuddled.
Don't pig-out on what-ifs and whys.
Just taste of God's goodness
each morning
and don't swallow fear's bitter lies.

A Prayer for Everyday

This new day dawns
with challenges
at home and on the job.
But lest I quit before I start,
please hear this prayer, dear God.

Today I ask
that I may see
Your hand in all I do.
I need Your help
to trust Your heart
until this day is through.

Please help me, Lord,
to be Your ears
to those not always heard.
And may I listen
with an eye
to speak a loving word.

On Foggy Days

On dank and dismal foggy days,
when your vision is less than 20/20,
God's ways are difficult to discern.
It's in times like these
that we learn to trust what we cannot see
and practice the faith we profess.

I'd be the first to confess
these aren't the easiest of days.
On such dreaded days,
we feel like God doesn't care
(if He even hears us).
But He does.

And He is committed to restoring our vision
when the fog lifts and the sun appears
and His purposes are once again made clear.

But till then we go forward,
living one day at a time,
waiting for reasons
and poems that rhyme
(and learning to live by faith).

*I battle discouragement on a regular basis. Earlier in my
ministry I was diagnosed with clinical depression. Gratefully, I
climbed out of the basement of emotional despair with a keener
sense of the human condition and a determination to express it
with descriptive words.*

Hugged By God

"I need a hug!" I told the Lord
"I'm lonely and afraid."
I long for arms to comfort me
and that is why I prayed.

My friends know I am hurting so.
My family feels my pain.
But only God can hold me close
when I'm alone again.

He shelters me from sorrow's chill.
He shields me when I'm weak.
The arms of God sustain me when
I'm too stressed out to speak.

Enveloped in His strong embrace,
I know I can go on.
If hugged by God, I'll find the means
to face what's still to come.

Rest Assured

When you aren't sure what God's doing,
rest assured He's not asleep.
He is wide awake and watching.
He can see you when you weep.

He is moved by your dilemma
and He aches to feel your pain.
But He just wants you to trust Him
when it's easier to blame.

If you welcome each tomorrow
as a gift sent just for you,
He'll surprise you with His presence
and the peace you long for, too.

Lord, I'm Praying

Lord, I'm praying. Can you hear me?
I am helplessly in need.
Overwhelmed and over-burdened.
Understand me. Feel me bleed.

Lord, I'm praying. Are You listening?
You're not answering my prayers.
But You promised asking matters.
Please convince me that You care.

Lord, I'm praying. Don't ignore me.
I feel desperately afraid.
I have no one else to turn to.
Make me grateful that I prayed.

I Prayed for You Today

Even though I wasn't sure
exactly what to say,
I talked to God and spoke your name.
I prayed for you today.
I asked the Lord
to give you strength,
to calm you from your stress,
to free you from the things you fear
and bathe your mind with rest.
I asked the Lord to help you
in the uphill days to come.
I asked our precious loving God
to complete what He's begun.
He whispered in the quiet
and filled my heart with peace.
He said that you are deeply loved,
and that His love won't cease.

A Cup of Life

Our lives are like a cup of tea.
At least that's how it seems to me.
It's bold and sweet and tastes the best
when sipped with those you love.

It has to steep to turn out great.
But life, like tea, is worth the wait.
Though, if we're honest, we'd admit
delays are sometimes hard.

Like fragile China porcelain,
our bodies, marred and chipped by sin,
are delicate and prone to crack
and will eventually break.

But when our lives at last are through ,
the grace of God, like Super Glue,
will mend the shards that were our cups
and fill us with new life.

It's all because of Calvary
where Innocence, poured out like tea,
emptied Himself of Heaven's Blend
and drank what we deserved.

A One-Word Prayer

I just breathe the name of *Jesus*
when my heart is filled with fear.
And though I cannot see His face,
I know that He is near.

When I whisper *Jesus* softly
I'm admitting I'm in need.
By calling out that precious name,
my stress-bound soul is freed.

It's a one-word prayer I utter
when I'm not sure what to pray.
It's a prayer of sweet surrender
when I'm weary of "my way."

I pray *Jesus* when I'm worried
or when I am depressed.
I say *Jesus* when my mind's confused
or when my life's a mess.

It's a prayer He always answers
as He gives me eyes to see
the proof of His sweet presence
and His tender love for me.

Disabled by Sin

I'm disabled by sin, Holy Father.
Paralyzed by my self-centered will.
I can't feel You around me.
I am blind to Your love,
handicapped by my limping resolve.

I'm especially needy, dear Father.
A special-needs child I am.
But braced by Your grace
I am ready to stand.
Would You steady me
with Your strong hand?

Would You carry me,
wash me, forgive me?
I long to be spiritually whole.
And though I am weak
and will fall yet again,
I give You my heart and my soul.

Time for a Faith Lift

Over-stressed,
I'm feeling anxious.
Lord, I'm rumpled
in and out.

What was smooth
is now quite wrinkled.
Trust has fallen prey
to doubt.

I could use
a faith-lift, Father.
Reconstruct
my downcast glance.
Fix my gaze
on what You've promised
so my countenance
can dance.

Where It All Began

Just remember where it all began
when you doubt the things that God has planned,
when the future seems uncertain
and the past seems so unfair.

When you're prone to feel discouraged
and you don't have any courage left
to reach the goals God gave you,
don't give in to your despair.

When you find you lack real feeling
and you need an inner healing,
just review where God has brought you
and give thanks for what He's done.

Unwrap the Present

As if dangling from a spider's web,
our lives hang by a slender thread.
Our health is fragile
no matter how agile
or fit we think we may be.
And dreams shatter.
Plans change.
Death shows up unannounced.
So pounce on each moment
and unwrap the present
and learn how to number your days
(that you may gain a heart of wisdom
and live each day as a gift from the Lord).

A Seven Word Prayer

Help me, Lord, I really need You.
I don't think I can go on.
I am weak and growing weaker.
My reserves are all but gone.

Help me, Lord, I really need You.
Hypertension robs my sleep.
Feeling helplessly immobile,
I can barely even speak.

Help me, Lord, I really need You.
I'm imprisoned by my fears.
I am paralyzed by worry
and my future's so unclear.

Help me, Lord, I really need You.
Seven words but just one plea.
I'm a child who needs a Father.
Fix Your gaze, O God, on me.

The Brace of God's Grace

You questioned God,
"Is faith a fraud?"
The Lord seemed far away.
Without your son,
your life was done.
Your grief consumed each day.

But then time passed.
And like a cast,
God held your heart in place.
Though fractured deep,
you ceased to weep.
God's grace was like a brace.

And here you are
with tissue scarred,
but healing nonetheless.
I think of you.
I often do
and pray that you'll be blessed.

You've Got Mail!

My laptop spoke to me today
as I clicked AOL.
A voice that I have come to love
responded, "You've got mail!"

Before my eyes a list appeared,
derived from cyberspace.
And as I opened what was sent,
I witnessed God's sweet grace.

WEEKDAYS

One e-mail came from my dear dad
who's plagued by chronic pain.
He simply said he'd prayed for me
and hoped I'd do the same.

Another came from one I know
whose wife walked out last year.
He told me how he'd found the Lord.
His words were most sincere.

And then a guy I've never met
surprised me with a note.
He said he'd found encouragement
from something that I wrote.

A screen name I had never seen
intrigued me so I clicked.
It was a poem aimed to heal
the hurts of those heartsick.

A widow from our church e-mailed
to say she'd been quite low.
But then she said she'd found a friend
and thought I'd like to know.

Each e-mail felt as though the Lord
were messaging to me.
I was affirmed and filled with faith
as I read prayerfully.

And so when I hear "You've got mail!"
you shouldn't think it odd
that I perk up and sit right down,
prepared to hear from God.

Slurping Worry Soup

Are you anxious, stressed and frazzled?
No offense, but you look pooped.
And the cause may be your diet.
Are you slurping worry soup?

Is your stomach roped and knotted?
Are you often out of breath?
If you are, you're in big trouble.
Such a plight could lead to death.

Please dismount and hold your horses.
Take the saddle off each steed.
You've been going like a racehorse,
serving God at breakneck speed.

But your service won't be lengthy
if your health you disregard.
Lo, the price for stressed-out living
is expensive. It is hard.

Quit your braying and start praying.
Ask the Lord to slow you down.
Saddle up the old gray mare.
Take a trail ride out of town.

Slowly saunter in the meadow.
Mosey off and get alone.
Spend a day attuned to silence.
Leave your laptop and your phone.

Ride old Nellie home at sunset.
Take your time and brush her coat.
If you spend a day unplugging,
you will find that you can cope.

Bound and Gagged

My stomach needs a Boy Scout.
It's all tangled up in knots.
Ropes of stress are coiled within me
And my fraying nerves are shot.

Anxious worries hold me hostage.
I am gagged and shackle-bound.
Truth be told, I need a SWAT team.
What is missing must be found.

What needs finding is contentment,
Inner calm and peace of mind.
I am cuffed by haunting deadlines.
Lacking focus, I am blind.

Stress imprisons. It's a killer—
Should I call the FBI?
This kidnapper is most-wanted.
If not caught, I just might die.

"Who will rescue me?" I pleaded.
"Who will save me from myself?
I am longing for my freedom.
I am sick, in need of health."

Then I heard a still voice whisper.
"Cool your jets. Chill out and breathe.
I, the Lord, will bust your stressors.
Just be patient and believe."

Let's Hear It for Knee Mail

Prayer's like texting God in Heaven
with my worries and requests.
Into cyberspace I venture
with those things that cause me stress.

On my knees I am reminded
God is on my buddy list.
He's a friend who cares and listens
unlike some from whom I'm dissed.

I spell out my need for wisdom
as I spill out inner angst
While I wait for God to answer,
I'm inclined to text him THANKS!

E-mail from Heaven.

Timeless truths in an instant message.

If Heaven offered free e-mail.
what would our loved ones want to tell?
Since they now know what matters most,
I'm guessing they would write...

To view each day as if a gift.
To run t'ward peace when there's a rift.
To see the value when we play.
To know God hears us when we pray.

To recognize there's always time
to bend an ear or to be kind.
To smell the fragrance of a flower.
To bask beneath a summer shower.

To feel the wonder of it all
when autumn leaves begin to fall.
To taste the sweetness of a pear.
To give to God our every care.

To serve a homeless man a meal
and then to journal what we feel.
To stroke a newborn baby's hand
in awe of God's mysterious plans.

To watch the ocean churn and foam.
To take a sunrise walk alone.
To stand beside a dying friend
and hold their hand until the end.

To understand that life is brief,
marked both by joy and also grief.
To come to terms with Jesus Christ,
acknowledging His sacrifice.

To baptize Doubt as Faith's godchild
who will (in time) believe.

Redeeming a Sleepless Night

In the early morning hours
when you cannot fall asleep,
try conversing with the Shepherd.
Don't rely on counting sheep.

Take advantage of the silence
as you toss and turn in vain.
Try to verbalize your feelings
as you pray in Jesus' name.

Close your eyes and praise the Savior.
Hum a song you've sung in church.
And you'll sense the Lord beside you
on your horizontal perch.

Late Night Options

Every night you get to choose:
The Bible or the late-night news?
Scripture helps you to relax.
The news will cram your mind with facts
like death counts in a bloody war
or who held up your corner store.

The news gives cause for counting sheep
before you close your eyes in sleep.
But reading adds weight to your eyes
while helping you become more wise.

If, just before you hit the hay,
you watch the heartache of the day,
your nervous system starts to race!
The muscles in your arms and face
betray the fact that you're uptight
and make you anxious through the night.

But if, when your long day is through,
you sit and turn a page or two,
you give your stressors time to chill
and cut your worries down to nil.

It seems so easy, yet it's not.
It's hard to break routines you've got.
But change is worth its weight in gold
if you don't let stress keep its hold.

Praying with the Prime Minister

Number 10 on Downing Street
is now the Brown Hotel.
The Blairs are out, the Browns are in,
and we Yanks wish them well.

A Church of Scotland manse was home
to Gordon long ago.
This PM was a PK once
in pea-green wet Glasgow.

A preacher's kid? in Parliament?
Prime Minister, no less?
Let's pray that means he talks with God
when struggling with stress.

But prayer is not just for PMs;
It works for everyone.
The angst of life is less intense
when bedtime prayers are done.

God listens to the Brits and Dutch,
the Greeks and stoic Swedes.
He hears the prayers of Africans,
the Persians and the Medes,

the Chinese and Peruvians
the Indians and Fins
the Japanese, Koreans too.
All women and all men.

So whether you're on Downing Street
or Main Street USA,
just give the Lord your heart's concerns,
and let Him guide your way.

Christ's Bride in Baghdad

It seems they're bombing Christians now.
God help us! Help them! Holy cow!
In Baghdad those who follow Christ
are symbols of the West.
They're viewed as just extensions of
one nation with its hawks and doves.
And since they are it's likely more
will be put to the test.

The Church is not that prevalent
where Islam's made its major dent.
But where the faithful worship Christ,
His cross can still be found.
Though homemade bombs and hand grenades
must give them cause to be afraid,
the Bride of One they call their Groom
will worship underground.

The Key to Unlocking Hall Closets

From Swaggart to Haggard
from Adam to the cross,
when we face up to who we are
we realize the cost.

"Be sure your sins will find your out!"
our mothers used to say.
And though we tried to hide our guilt,
the night gives way to day.

The light reveals what we have hid.
The closet door won't close.
Those dirty secrets stuffed inside
will finally be exposed.

The key is keeping closets clean
by dusting them each day.
Examining ourselves, a must
confessing as we pray.

Let Jesus have the closet key.
He longs to look inside.
He wants to cleanse you of your lust,
your passions, greed and pride.

Don't gloat about another's sin,
though tempting that may be.
Except but for the grace of God,
Ted Haggard might be thee.

The White House is Over-Rated

Who lives inside the White House?
God doesn't care that much.
He's more concerned with who is living
in your house... and such.

A house that has inhabitants
who start each day in prayer
will help protect our much-loved land
from evil acts of terror.

A godly man and woman
who will bravely take a stand,
impact our nation's character
far more than just one man.

If in our homes faith's not divorced
from public policy,
God has the means to bring about
the ends He longs to see.

So if your choice for President
did not survive his fight,
remember it's your house that counts
far more than one that's White.

Praying with Matt Lauer

While waking up from yesterday
I sip some joe and greet Today.
From Matt, Ann, Meredith and Al,
I learn what I should know.

I have to watch the news each dawn
to find out all that has gone on
while I've been comatose to life,
asleep upon my bed.

In Asia, markets have declined.
In Munich, prisoners once confined
successfully escaped from jail
and now are fugitives.

In Ireland, a deadly bomb
killed five young children and their mom.
And off the coast of Haiti,
there's a hurricane in sight.

What happens while I'm fast asleep
amounts to more than counted sheep.
The world can change in eight short hours.
That's why I stay informed.

But with the sadness everywhere,
I watch the news and say a prayer
in which I ask God's will be done
on earth just like in Heaven.

** Since we were married in 1982, my wife and I have begun
most mornings having our devotions along with a cup of coffee
and then watching The Today Show to catch up on what
transpired in the world overnight.*

A Prayer in Hard Times

This recession-based depression
has me calling for a shrink.
When some banks default
and stocks go bust,
I don't know what to think.

Worried sick that my investments
may grow worthless overnight,
I ask You, Lord,
to help me see
my net worth from Your sight.

Shift my focus to Your blessings
such as health and family
and the knowledge
that You show Your love
to me abundantly.

Birth Pangs of a Cosmic Sort

There're wars, earthquakes and tidal waves.
Then deadly aftershocks.
Could Armageddon be on deck?
So ask newsmen on Fox.

And hurricanes are on the rise
with killer floods in tow.
There's talk of bird flu and mad cow.
St. Helens's set to blow.

A Carpenter from Nazareth
once hammered home the truth
that escalating tragedies
would wake prophetic sleuths.

So could the end be drawing close
for late great planet Earth?
Are all these headlines labor pains
that mark redemption's birth?

We can't be sure, but let's beware.
The Scriptures make it clear.
That Carpenter will come again.
Perhaps this is the year.

There's Within My Heart a Malady

There's within my heart a malady.
Arteries quite clogged with plaque.
I'm a time bomb waiting to explode
from a massive heart attack.

Refrain:
Jesus, Jesus, Jesus,
help me stay alive.
Even if I'm coded blue, dear Lord,
promise me that I'll survive.

Once my life was marked by balanced meals.
I went jogging every day.
Over time I lost my discipline
and that's why I'm heard to pray. (*Refrain*)

Soon the medics will be at my door,
hoping they can bring me back.
After doing CPR on me,
with their panels they will zap. (*Refrain*)

But perhaps there's time to change my ways,
starting with the things I eat.
Saying no to French fries and ice cream,
I'll say yes to lean, white meat. (*Refrain*)

(tune: He Keeps Me Singing)

A Time Management Confession

I must confess I'm always tardy.
Late to church or to a party.
Late for lunch with those I love
and late to Starbucks, too.

I'm late at work and on vacation.
I hate this well-earned reputation.
My doctor and my dentist know
I never show on time.

I'm like the Wonderlandish rabbit,
a victim of a dreadful habit.
I'm late for all important dates
while others wait for me.

I know it's selfish and unkind,
but that's not why I lag behind.
What screws me up is thinking
I can squeeze in one more thing.

And then I fail to estimate
just how much time that task will take.
Then when at last it's finally done,
I'm late for what is next.

Oh, Father God, as You can see,
I've earned Your wrath. Please pity me.
I'm asking for a second chance
and minutes by the hour.

Ground-Zero Faith

When it seems you've been blindsided
and you crumble from within,
let the Lord be your strong tower.
He will shield you once again.

When it seems like God is missing
and your faith cannot be found,
don't suspend your search as useless.
Where you are is holy ground.

When both doubt and fear attack you
and your will to trust gives way,
don't just stand there in the rubble.
Humbly kneel and start to pray.

When your dreams lie in the ashes
and your confidence is gone,
don't despair about the future.
With God's help you can go on.

Footprints in the Sand

Wash over me, dear Father,
with the power of the sea.
Flood me with a sense of peace
that comes from only Thee.

As the undertow of panic
seeks to suck my courage down,
would You cause Your mighty waves
to beach me where I'm safe and sound?

And then as You have done before,
please do it once again,
please carry me within Your arms,
making footprints in the sand.

The Joy's in the Climb

It's not on the summit
where faith tends to grow.
We learn how to trust
in the valley below.

The trek is what matters.
The joy's in the climb,
as we practice God's presence
one day at a time.

A Family Prayer

Creator of our family tree
(especially the branch called me),
please let our roots grow deep and strong
so it will stand secure.

From limb to limb our tree has grown.
And, Lord, You've seen how winds have blown.
But by Your grace life's storms could not
uproot what You preserve.

Allow the blossoms on our tree
to scent our world most fragrantly.
And may the fruit that we will bear
help nourish those You love.

The Sandwich Generation Blues

We're the sandwich generation.
Launching children, nursing folks.
And the stress is no baloney,
though it's often grist for jokes.

It's a sandwich we must muster,
though we have a constant beef.
Teenage kids can be real turkeys
and our parents cause us grief.

Cut in half by what's demanded,
we're inclined to fall apart.
It's so hard to be a sandwich
squeezed by those who fill our hearts.

Lettuce ask the Lord to help us.
Life can spread us awfully thin
as we're chewed up by what eats us.
We're called heroes when we win.

** I wrote this on behalf of those like my wife and I who are
caring for the needs of aging parents while attempting to
launch their children.*

An Invitation to Dance

He looked at me and said, "Let's dance."
"I'll lead, just lean on me."
But I protested to the Lord:
"I'm clumsy. Can't you see?"

"I've two left feet. I don't know how.
I think I'd trip or fall.
I'd rather sit and sip some punch.
I just don't dance, that's all."

But He refused to turn away.
He winked at me and said,
"This is our song. Don't sit it out.
Come dance with Me instead."

Reluctantly, I took His hand.
I stood up as He smiled.
And in His arms my fears took wings.
I giggled liked a child.

We waltzed across the ballroom floor.
With grace He took the lead.
I didn't know which way to turn,
yet didn't feel the need.

I leaned my head upon His arm
and felt His strong embrace.
I knew He wouldn't let me go
or fall flat on my face.

Though lost in wonder, love and joy,
I found myself that night.
What I had feared for all those years,
became my soul's delight.

To think I'd almost missed it all.
Thank God, I took a chance
when He invited me to risk
by asking me to dance.

A God for All Seasons

In every season of my days
when I am stressed or prone to praise,
I'll hope in God's deliberate ways
to guide me through life's mazes.

When joy explodes within my mind
and faith seems easy (almost blind),
I'll worship Him in whom I find
a constant, true companion.

When skeptics shake my confidence
and cause my faith to sigh and wince,
I'll look to heaven's righteous Prince
to help me doubt my doubting.

When health declines and leaves me ill
and pain persists in spite of pills,
I'll trust my Father's perfect will,
embracing what's before me.

When worry robs what God intends
to fill my heart when my life ends,
I'll count on Him to be my friend
and give me grace for dying.

The Dash of Life

There is a dash on granite stones
that punctuates a yard of bones.
Unlike the dash we raced as kids,
it separates two dates.

This dash is not a race to run.
It speaks of all the things we've done.
It symbolizes how we've lived.
Our joys and our regrets.

This dash is not a pinch of salt.
It speaks of times we were at fault
and other times when we excelled
at helping those in need.

That little dash is just a line
that stands for how we spent our time.
And like our dash, our time is short
so make it count today.

A Prayer for a Struggling Friend

Before the night gave way to day
you came to mind and so I prayed
that God would fill your anxious heart
with confidence and peace.

You've battled such a long, long time
and I have never heard you whine
because you know that God's in charge
and He won't let you down.

And likely you must fight some more
to face some treatments yet in store.
So don't give up or trade your joy.
Emotions often lie.

Just whisper to the Lord your need.
That very act is but a seed
that sprouts within your doubting soul
and blossoms into hope.

It's not a petty thing at all
although some think prayer off the wall.
To talk to God is what works best
when we feel at our worst.

The Master Garment Maker

The Master Garment Maker
always knows what He's about
as He fashions, sews and finishes
a plan I sometimes doubt.

Though He chooses threads and fabrics
that to me seem quite absurd,
He's committed to a pattern
that's consistent with His Word.

If I trust the Garment Maker
as He mends my rips and frays,
I'll be clothed with what is needed
for some future cold, dark days.

Hold On to Your Dreams

There were dreams in your heart
the Lord planted and grew.
But, then something happened
and before long you knew

what you'd longed for and prayed
would in time come to pass,
became futile and hopeless.
Your dreams became dashed.

How you wished that your family
would walk with the Lord.
How you planned that your business
would sprout wings and soar.

You had hoped that you'd find
just the right place to serve,
but the Lord appeared absent.
Had He thrown you a curve?

You had dreamed of a mission
that would take you abroad.
It seemed you were called
but, alas, where was God?

And where was that healing
you prayed would be yours
when racked by depression
or riddled with sores?

Sometimes it must seem
that your journey's been wrong
when your dreams are delayed
and your heart's lost its song.

But lest you grow jaded
and give up your goals,
keep trusting, believing
the Lord's in control.

Death Bed Watch

I stand beside your bedside weeping,
comforted to see you sleeping.
While awake you're victimized by pain
that saps your peace.

I can't help thinking as I stand here,
how you rescued me from danger
when my nightmares bucked me off
and left me all alone.

I think about when you were standing
by my bed with bars of candy.
I was only six or seven,
home from school and sick.

But now it's my turn to be standing
at your bed. It's not demanding.
It's a privilege. Dad, I love you
more than you could know.

I stand beside your bedside weeping,
comforted to see you sleeping.
I am asking God to give you
dreams of Heaven's joys.

** I wrote this as my dad lay dying after a fourteen-year battle
with prostate cancer. As he slept, God gave me a picture of the
eternal rest that soon would be his.*

Crying for a Sick Grandpa

I know your grandpa's on your mind.
I know you're hurting so.
You're sad because you love him lots
and want to let him know.

What happened caught you by surprise.
You want to ask God why.
You want to tell Him it's not fair.
But all you do is cry.

You want to climb in Grandpa's lap.
You want to hear him speak.
You want to wake him up and play.
That's why your eyelids leak.

God sees the teardrops on your face.
He loves your grandpa, too.
God has a plan we will not see
until all this is through.

I pray God helps you sleep tonight
and gives you "Grandpa dreams."
I'm asking God to prove He's close
in spite of how it seems.

The Lord IS really in control.
Your grandpa's in good hands.
In time we'll know why this took place.
Someday we'll understand.

The Time is Near

Some doctors say your time is near,
but what that means to me is clear.
A time to hope and not give in.
A time for faith to grow within.

A time for walking with the Lord
and trusting Him for what's in store.
A time for standing on God's Word
with confidence your prayers are heard.

A time for sitting with your tea
and thanking God for family.
A time for kneeling at your bed
to give the Lord the fears you dread.

A time for lying still at night
and knowing things will be alright.
A time for grasping every day,
including ones when skies are gray.

A time for reading a good book
content to let another cook.
A time for laughing at a joke
and spending time until you're broke.

A time for getting extra rest
and taking stock of how you're blest.
A time for sharing your beliefs
without concern for critics' beefs.

So when you hear the time is near,
don't be dismayed or start to fear.
Those words are just a way to say
you've got the means to seize the day.

While I Can

I won't always have the chance to say
just what you mean to me.
We aren't guaranteed tomorrow
or each other's company.

We assume there'll be a next time,
but that's not always the case.
Health can break and dreams can shatter
like a priceless heirloom vase.

Unexpected circumstances
can derail our hoped-for plans.
So I'll let you know my feelings.
I will share them while I can.

Cry for My Son with Me

Oh, Lord, I feel so all alone.
Please let me know that You're aware.
At times You seem so far from my cry.
Cry. Now there's a familiar word.
Yes, I've done my share.
And wouldn't You when life's unfair?
Or don't you care what happens to those we love?
You say You do. And I know it's true (deep down).
This broken world of sin
defined by and drugs and cancer
breaks Your heart.
And in Your love, You gave Your answer.
You allowed Your young innocent to suffer and die
to prove how much You care.
From His lifeless broken body

hanging hopelessly from a cross,
hope (like blood) trickled down those Roman timbers.
Reaching the ground it flowed
around the globe like glue.
Yes, our broken world is held together
(much like my fragile broken heart)
by the hope that speaks of healing yet to come.
Come quickly, Lord Jesus!
But in the meantime,
won't You cry for my son with me?

* My wife and I have three daughters, no sons. I wrote this for a man and woman in our community whose twenty-something son died in a tragic set of circumstances. This was my attempt to encourage them with the fact that God identified with their pain.

Shoes

From those booties when we're babies
to those slippers when we're old,
foot apparel make a statement.
Sometimes subtle, often bold.

Slip-on loafers or Adidas,
spiky heels or rubber soles,
what we wear below our ankles
tells a story heaven knows.

Shoes remind us to be patient
with the ones with whom we talk.
They've been scuffed by pain and sorrow
as with God they've tried to walk.

Hidden Treasure

When you hide the living Word of God
down deep inside your heart,
those ancient words within a book
do more than make you smart.

They motivate obedience.
They give you cause to pray.
They guide the way you think and act
or how you work and play.

When Scripture is internalized,
God's Spirit is released
to fill your life with needed joy
and leave your faith increased.

The Gospel According to Baseball

It's a game that's based on bases,
first and second, third and home.
And the rules remain consistent
whether played in Rome or Nome.

You must first head straight to first base.
You can't skip it or take third.
Without rules there'd be no meaning.
Without rules games are absurd.

And the game of life's no different.
Those who play it on their own
think that they can skip the bases
and then slide in late at home.

But there's order to the process.
We must take each stage in stride.
Someone pitches us the Gospel
and explains why Jesus died.

First we must accept forgiveness
that He gave us on the cross.
After that it's on to second
where we let Him be the boss.

Then we're third-base bound by serving
those around us who have needs.
And it's likely we'll remain there
till we've lost our pride and greed.

Then in time our Coach will motion
that it's time to head for home.
That's the time we'll know we made it,
as the King smiles from His throne.

So the moral of this poem
is to let the game you love
help you understand the ground rules
that apply to what's above.

A Great-Commission Church

The Great Commission
remains our mission.
It's what defines our cause.
To reach the lost at any cost
is Heaven's royal law.

And when we go
the world will know
the good news of God's grace.
By easing pain in Jesus' name,
we give His love a face.

We Bring Our World to Christ

We bring our world to Christ because He loves it.
A world for which He suffered, bled and died.
A world of pain known by first names and faces
with fragile egos, anxious hopes and pride.
A world unreached with knowledge of salvation.
A generation we've been called to serve.

We bring our world to Christ through acts of friendship.
A listening ear, a hand that reaches out.
Making the time to get to know our neighbors.
Discovering their passions, fears and doubts.
Extending mercy when their hearts are broken.
Transparently acknowledging our pain.

We bring our world to Christ, convinced He'll use us.
Just as we are, we're partners in His plan.
We choose to be the salt and light He called us,
creating thirst for God in our dark land.
We bring our world to Christ, anticipating
the varied ways He'll choose to answer prayer.

(tune: Finlandia)

Fresh and Clean

The washcloth of God's cleansing love
has scrubbed me from my sin.
I am all clean. My guilt is gone.
I'm "Downey fresh" within.

The shampoo of His soapy grace
conditions tangled lives.
The fragrance of a second chance
suggests that I can thrive.

The toothbrush of God's timeless truth
prevents my soul's decay.
By heeding what the Bible says,
I start brand new each day.

Recovery: A Lifelong Journey
In celebration of the road less traveled.

A road to freedom
(in spite of the inevitable potholes
and flat tires).

A path of forgiveness
(both of others and yourself).

A street of dreams
(bypassing those all-too-familiar
nightmarish dead ends).

A freeway of new beginnings
(devoid of those dreaded tollbooths
that marked the old way).

An on-ramp to Transformation Turnpike
(that allows immediate access
no matter where you are).

A parkway of beauty
(where you rediscover
the indescribable wonder of nature).

A route of peace
(that leads beyond external happiness
to inner contentment).

A highway of hope
(where the rear-view mirror
gives way to the windshield).

A lifelong journey
(where the trip is as meaningful
as the destination).

** The above poem is dedicated to countless friends who have
made the courageous decision, with God's help, to acknowledge
addictions and self-destructive patterns of behavior in order
to begin the lifelong journey on the road called "recovery," one
day at a time.*

Litter in Its Place

Discarded, crumpled litter.
A life that's trashed and tossed.
Some say it's only garbage
and others call it lost.

But is it refuse? Really?
When garbage meets God's grace,
grace redefines its value,
and puts litter in its place.

** I wrote this little rhyme in anticipation of my friend Michael
Medved, film critic and radio personality, speaking at our
church. Michael is a crusader for cleaning up our environment.
Thanks to his contagious passion, I have become more litter-
conscious.*

Longing for the Good Old Days

The way it was is gone for good,
but it was awfully good back then.
No wonder we are always quick
to ask "remember when?"

We savored life. We thanked the Lord,
even though those times were tough.
We didn't have what we have now,
but we all had enough.

We scrimped and saved to get ahead,
but we mostly stayed behind.
Still, neighbors knew when we had needs
and helped us in a bind.

The good old days found us in church.
We made sure that we were there.
We were one nation under God
so we took time for prayer.

But now it seems we're backwards-prone.
We are wealthy, but we're poor.
We've little time for those we love,
while jobs we hate take more.

But since we can't rewind the tape
to those days of yesteryear,
let's make the most of time God gives
and cherish those we're near.

The Road Ahead

What's still to come need not be feared,
though you can't see ahead.
And when life's storms mean slippery roads,
you're guaranteed good tread.

The Word of God is like a sign
that points to what's in store.
It helps you to slow down and turn
your focus to the Lord.

Though shadows fall across your way,
the darkness won't last long.
There's beauty in this trip called life.
Each day find Nature's song.

Christ, You are Welcome

Christ, You are welcome in this heart of mine.
Come be my house-guest, O Savior divine.
Warmed by Your presence, Doubt's chill will depart.
Step through the threshold and enter my heart.

Walk through each room in my life, Lord, with me.
Point out the structural damage you see.
Do what is needed to re-make my space.
Remove the refuse, fill each room with Your grace.

Here is the title, I give it to You.
My heart's Your home; Let Your glory shine through.
Make me Your dwelling. Live Your life in me.
My heart's Your home, Lord. Your love is the key.

(tune: Be Thou My Vision)

*I had the privilege of having one of Dr. Robert Boyd
Munger's final classes at Fuller Seminary He is the one who
wrote the little booklet "My Heart, Christ's Home." The above
is based on that timeless devotional classic.*

A String of Pearls

Our stories are pearls that just beg to be strung.
They're lyrics of living that long to be sung.
They're proof of a faithful and purposeful God
whose plans are best seen in a mirror.

Our stories are treasures that must be unearthed.
They're priceless possessions that point to our worth.
They're scripts of God's drama in which we've been cast
and in which His goodness is staged.

Our stories are echoes recalling His voice.
They're snapshots of times we gave in to His choice.
They're mileage markers on life's winding trail
that celebrate how far we've come.

A Dialogue About Stress

Did you know that stress can kill you?
Are you kidding? *No, I'm not.*
It's a fact that nonstop worry
can constrict your veins a lot.

But I thought that stress was helpful
to assure you do your best.
I've been told that nerves will help you
as you try to ace a test.

Well, a little goes a long way—
Sweaty palms and racing heart.
But relying on adrenaline . . .
That is when big problems start.

Hey, you talk like I'm an addict,
as if stress is like cocaine.
Well, it is! Stress is an upper,
but it brings you down again.

It can take you six feet under,
leave you motionless and cold.
And if somehow you survive it,
you'll be prematurely old.

Are you looking at my wrinkles?
And that tremor in your hands.
Hey, there's dandruff on your shoulders!
Okay, stop—I understand.

I confess that I'm addicted
to a life out of control.
And I know I'm slowly dying;
There's no joy inside my soul.

WEEKDAYS

Help me somehow to quit stressing.
I can't do it without aid.
Yes, I know. You are a hostage
to the choices you have made.

But there's hope if you are willing.
Just admit you're tired of stress.
Then cut way back on your "have-to's";
You can learn to live with less.

Do you mean cancel appointments?
Leave my briefcase in the car?
Now you're talking! That's the spirit!
Where you're headed's not that far.

But expect to have some setbacks.
When you stop your nonstop ways,
you'll feel as though something's missing.
But it's only just a phase.

Will I have to pray more often?
What about more exercise?
Should I plan on sleeping longer?
That would certainly be wise.

And try learning to say something
that will curb adrenal flow.
I'm convinced you'd be less stressed out
if more often you'd say "no!"

* Dr. Archibald Hart taught at Fuller Seminary when I was a
student. His research has revealed how stressed-out individuals
become addicted to their own adrenalin.

The Edge of Adventure

When God brings you to the brink, you think
there's not much cause to hope.
It is clear that there's a drop-off.
There's no path and you've no rope.

If you jumped, you wouldn't make it.
Kinda looks like life is through.
But if you will just be patient,
God in time will rescue you.

Such occasions call for trusting
and that goes against our grain.
We don't like what faith requires;
no firm answers, sometimes pain.

All the same, God can be trusted.
He won't leave you on the brink.
Don't put all your stock in feelings
or in what at times you think.

Put your weight on what God's promised.
Lean on Him and do not fear.
Though it's scary where you're standing,
ask for courage. God is near.

The Dark Knight with a Troubled Soul

Heath's ledger proved the bottom line
is more than fame or Oscar's shine.
The Joker knows (what soon all will)
there's more that must add up.

The dark knight with a troubled soul
will give account for his life's goals.
But that is true for all of us
when we face Judgment Day.

The "good life" isn't all that bad
and yet Heath seemed so often sad.
This Brokeback wrangler played a gay,
but lacked a lasting joy.

The "good life" (even with good works)
won't compound in eternal perks.
All ledgers will be audited
with just one thing in mind.

Did you accept God's sinless Son
before your time on earth was done?
Don't take a chance.
Spurned grace means Hell.
And then the joke's on you.

The Second Exodus

In May of 1948
the Promised Land became a state
as exiled Jews (dispersed) returned,
reclaiming what God gave.

From nations of the world they came,
united by a common aim.
To build a home and make a life
where milk and honey flow.

It was a second Exodus
that gave The Jews good cause to trust
a gracious God who keeps His word
while doubters stand amazed.

God used David Ben-Gurion
to call the sons of Abraham
back to The Land where faith was born
and Isaac was redeemed.

It truly was a miracle
that we should take time to recall,
for those who pray for Israel's peace
will know God's sweet shalom.

** This poem is dedicated to my friend, Dr. Abraham Kaplan,
whose acclaimed choral compositions celebrate the spirit of
those who settled modern-day Israel.*

A Call to Prayer for Our Troops

Our men and women in Iraq
are under stress and fierce attack.
They need our prayers regardless
how we feel about the war.

Defending freedom far from home,
our troops can sometimes feel alone,
and when their mission is maligned,
they wonder why they're there.

The risk is real as terror thrives.
Just add up all who've lost their lives
in liberating helpless ones
who dream of being free.

They're strong and brave, at times afraid.
But they take heart to hear we've prayed
for health and safety, faith and peace
and courage to keep on.

Don't let them down. It's up to us.
We're called to pray. We simply must.
Our gallant soldiers look to us
as we look to our God.

Waltzing with Faith

When we can't see what's 'round the bend
and don't know how this trip will end,
we have a chance to take a chance
and dance a waltz called faith.

Like Abraham, we're called to risk.
Suggestion? No! The Lord insists
that we jump with no parachute
and trust Him for what's next.

So, hey, let's dance and let God lead.
He knows exactly what we need
to see us to the journey's end
and so much more in store.

Retirement God's Way

Not retired! You're retreaded
for the journey yet ahead.
Find God's purpose and keep traveling.
Don't just veg until you're dead.

While it's fun to golf and garden
or to hunt for "early birds,"
don't just graze and take it easy
with the A A R P herds.

Joy is found in serving people.
You feel younger when you give.
Fill your free time with some meaning.
Don't become an empty sieve.

You were meant to make a difference
for as long as you're alive.
God intends that your retirement
be a time in which you thrive.

Let the Bible be your compass.
Steer your life toward those nearby.
Share your time and skills with others.
Don't just diddle till you die.

To Be His Arms

For those who volunteer in orphanages.

They long for love, to be embraced.
Their eyes reflect their hope.
Give them a smile, they give it back.
Deny them and they mope.

God's led you to befriend these kids.
To give them cause to trust.
You know you can't ignore their needs.
You have to go. You must.

Yours is a sacred ministry.
To serve in Jesus' name.
You have been called to be His arms.
It's such a simple aim.

Their world is filled with empty dreams.
Such sadness, pain and yet…
Your touch leaves God-prints in their hearts
and cushions their neglect.

Let's Hear It for Relation-ships!

Relation-ships comprise the fleet
that journeys toward God's best.
Armada-like they war against
a foe called loneliness.

Relation-ships will let you cruise
to longed-for ports of call
where joys are doubled, sorrows halved,
where fear-based hurdles fall.

Relation-ships need maintenance
to brave life's stormy seas.
You can't just let them sail at will,
relying on a breeze.

Relation-ships provide the deck
where honesty is lived.
It's on these vessels rocked by waves,
you learn to take and give.

Gibson's Fall from Grace

Jesus isn't Mel's sole passion.
Seems he has another thirst.
His rye humor isn't funny.
Guess the bottle's Gibson's curse.

Having tripped, the star's now tarnished.
Critics of his faith take aim.
Mel is now an easy target.
Such a fall has left him lame.

But before you start to judge him,
look inside your "righteous" gown.
Chances are you have your issues
that caused Christ his thorny crown.

Bathed in blood, we are forgiven.
Still we're flawed and prone to sin.
Every day we need God's power
to resist the beast within.

So before you act so smugly,
pray for Mel. Admit your need.
There but by God's grace we stumble,
tripped by ego, lust and greed.

** This was written after Mel Gibson, the director of the highly
acclaimed film, "The Passion of the Christ," was arrested for
driving under the influence*

.

Facing Final Jeopardy
Remembering Merv Griffin

A Lovely Bunch of Coconuts
Merv gave us long ago.
A Wheel of Fortune spun his way
with Pat and Vanna's show.

And Jeopardy was just his thing,
the answer/question swap.
It seemed that Griffin had the knack
to put Trebek on top.

For twenty years his daytime talk
(with Treacher by his side)
launched rising stars and made us laugh.
His ratings didn't slide.

But recently I heard the news
that made me want to cry.
Merv played his final hand on earth.
It was his turn to die.

Merv faced his final Jeopardy.
The answer was God's grace.
I hope he got the question right.
"What is life's final ace?"

A Book Called "Yourself"

So, what then will be your life story?
It's a book that you're writing each day.
You're unique, so I guess it's a novel.
Still, your future's a big mystery.

Your story is bound to be noticed
by those who observe what you write.
Will your words offer Christ-like compassion
with phrases of reasoned insight?

Will your sentences question the culture
as you challenge the lies it conveys?
Will your paragraphs stand out in bold print
as you stand up to ungodly ways?

Will your story be read by the masses?
Or will it be left on some shelf?
The things that you write
on each day's empty page
will result in a book called "Yourself."

A Different Kind of War
With gratitude for the Salvation Army

A soup line once kept folks alive
who otherwise would not survive.
And thanks to these in uniform,
a "soup line" still exists.

God warmed the heart of William Booth
and helped him understand the truth
that empty bellies have no ears
to hear they're really loved.

And General Booth enlisted those
who proudly wore their soldier clothes
and fought on front lines in the streets,
in alleys and skid rows.

His army fights a different war.
To love the addict, feed the poor,
to help the jobless find a skill
and give the homeless hope.

With Praise for Yawns

Don't think it rare that we need air.
It is our daily bread.
Without that unseen nourishment
we all would soon be dead.

So when a yawn is coming on,
don't fight it. Feed your face.
Our appetite for oxygen
is part of God's sweet grace.

So open wide. Those yawns provide
our hungry lungs with food.
That extra snack of oxygen
is anything but rude.

Tolerance vs. Truth

We Christians aren't so tolerant.
We pray for those who're gay.
And when it comes to knowing God,
we say there's just one way.

We claim the womb is where life starts,
that euthanasia's wrong.
That Mother Nature can't be raped
by spills that rob her song.

For us the Bible's most unique.
Unlike the other texts,
it's God's own Word to his sick world,
explaining why we're vexed.

The bottom line? We value truth
above blind tolerance.
For when infection threatens life,
a boil must be lanced.

Treasure in Life's Trash

Slumdog Millionaire offers truth you can bank on.

There's a movie getting rave reviews.
An indy film (quite rare)
about a kid who won big bucks.
It's *Slumdog Millionaire*.

It paints an abstract picture of
a truth that's most concrete.
The canvas of this arty flick
boasts something really neat.

Slumdog points out the rich reward
in what seems waste at best.
Misfortune's dung and what life deals
give answers to life's tests.

No heartache's wasted by our God.
He uses all we face.
Rejections, breakups, loss and pain
are gifts we can embrace.

For in each hurt we're offered hints
that help us move ahead.
Defeat's a lifeline in disguise.
Dead ends aren't really dead.

A treasure hides deep down inside
those things that cause despair.
I searched and found redemptive truth
in *Slumdog Millionaire*.

SPECIAL DAYS

Baby Talk

Do you know the world you've entered
is a planet scarred by war?
Do you have the slightest notion
how much blood's been spilled before?

Precious one, would it surprise you
if I told you what's ahead
will be difficult and lonely,
marked by pain until you're dead?

Nonetheless, my little child,
will you trust me when I say
that it's worth the grief you'll suffer
to embrace what comes your way?

Will you comprehend your trials
come to only make you strong?
Will you seek to do the right thing
but then learn from times you're wrong?

SPECIAL DAYS

As you sleep upon my shoulder,
what sweet dreams now fill your mind?
Are you dreaming of the fun we'll have
when you are eight or nine?

Can you picture playing baseball,
soccer games or ballet tights?
In your dreams are you just average
or (unlike me) very bright?

What's the path you'll one day journey?
To which jobs will you be drawn?
As you think about tomorrow,
what life goals will turn you on?

Can you feel me stroke your fingers
and plant kisses on your cheek?
Do you hear the Father's whispers
in the gentle words I speak?

Will I live to see your children?
Will you love me when I'm old?
Could it be there'll come a day when
you and I will reverse roles?

Who's to say my precious bundle?
Who can tell what years will bring?
But for now my little darling,
will you listen as I sing?

"My child you're cherished. Relax in my arms.
I pledge to protect you from danger and harm.
I'm awed by the wonder of your tiny frame
and wowed by the privilege to give you my name."

* The last four lines of this poem can be sung as a lullaby to the tune of "Away in a Manger."

Tiny Feet

Those tiny feet
you touch and stroke
amaze you with delight.
They'll one day grow
to walk and run
and stand for what is right.
Days and years will scurry by.
Time will seem to race.
Your little one will soon be gone.
So, guard each measured pace.

The Fruit of Love

The fruit of love, this gift of life,
we place, O God, within Your care.
To know Your grace and guiding hand
in years to come is now our prayer.

This little child is known by You.
Inclined to truth and evil too.
Would You protect this one we love
from sin and harm their whole life through?

This child's future waits with hope,
enveloped with the Spirit's grace.
Tomorrow's promise can be glimpsed
within this infant's tiny face.

With humble joy we recognize
a task that has only begun.
A sacred charge lies in our arms,
to cradle faith and pass it on.

We praise You Father God alone.
We praise You Jesus, Son of love.
And to the Spirit Holy One,
we sing our praise. Amen.

*Of the scores of hymn texts I have penned over the past thirty
years, this is the only one that has been published in a hymnal.*

A Grandparent's Reflections

These arms of mine have waited long
to hold you and to pray
that God would grace you with His love
and guide you in His way.

Most precious one, my child's child,
in your small face I see
your mother's mouth, your father's nose.
Perhaps that dimple's me.

One thing I know with certainty.
You're worth far more than gold.
And when I hold you, I feel rich
on days I'm feeling old.

GRADUATION

The Blessing

"The blessing" is the greatest gift
a dad and mom can give.
It says your child is special,
that the Lord said they should live.

It's a compass for the future
and it points to godly goals
as it guides our sons and daughters
on their journey of the soul.

"The blessing" says they're gifted,
they're amazing, most unique.
It says you see potential
in the interests that they seek.

It says you'll always love them.
That there's nothing they could do
that would cause you to rescind your love
even when their friends are few.

It's a crown of worth and beauty.
It's a robe of family pride.
It's an oath you speak on God's behalf
that says He's on their side.

A Charge to Graduates

Hey Graduate,

In 1 Timothy 4:12, Saint Paul wrote, "Don't let anyone
look down on you because you are young, but set an
example for the believers in speech, in life, in love, in
faith and in purity."

But what exactly does that verse from the Bible mean?

It means that even though you're young,
you really have the right
to show our culture how to live.
Paul's words are hardly trite.

They're timeless thoughts. They're right on track.
His words define your task
to live your lives in such a way
your friends are sure to ask

the reason for the hope you claim
in life beyond the grave,
or better yet, why when some fought,
you didn't, but forgave.

Paul calls you to resist the crowd
and how they look at sex.
To guard your thoughts, affections too,
by being circumspect.

And watch your mouth. Don't shade the truth.
When angry, do not swear.
Don't gossip or tell dirty jokes.
No biggie? Au contraire!

SPECIAL DAYS

That little rudder 'tween your teeth
can steer a battleship.
It is a spark that starts a fire
which through a forest rips.

Paul cautioned his friend Timothy
to flee temptation's pull.
He knew that if you flirt with sin,
you'll fail. And that's no bull!

Be quick to trust God's promises.
Be slow to doubt His heart.
The one who takes God at His Word,
will win because he's smart.

It all comes down to loving God
in big and little ways.
In how a person acts at school
or how that person plays.

To love the Lord means being kind
and putting others first
by canceling what you had planned
when someone's dreams have burst.

To love the Lord means hanging in
when others tend to bail.
It means to worship Him each week
so your faith won't grow stale.

There're two more ways your life in Christ
can remain fresh and pure.
Each day converse with Him through prayer
and read His Word for sure.

Well there you have it, graduate.
Take Saint Paul at his word.
You're not too young to live your faith
and model what you've heard.

Today is but a milepost.
Your journey's far from done.
In many ways, young friend of mine,
it's only just begun.

Commencement

The time has come to step out,
donning cap and gown, down the aisle
(an aisle I'll not soon forget).
For me, the thrill still lingers
of the day my fingers securely held
the diploma held out to me.
A band marked time with "Pomp and Circumstance"
as the procession began
while my parents applauded with pride.
And for you, my friend, the same awaits.
A robe of achievement (capping years of classes).
A sheepskin of survival. A handshake.
A smile. A party. Some gifts.
All this is God's gift to you.
Some call it graduation, but you will find it's more.
More than an ending, this day's a beginning,
when you commence toward what's still in store.
You see, the time has come to step out
and embrace a future God has planned.

New classes. New challenges.
New friends with which to meet them.
New ways to witness to your faith
beyond your parents' shadow.
New trails from which to choose.
So step out in full stride.
Commence the walk. And don't forget . . .
God wants to walk with you.

WEDDINGS

A Tux and Gown Night

You are dressed for success
as you promise your love,
and that's just what I'm wishing for you.
May you reach all your goals
as you live out your vows
and remain ever faithful and true.
On this tux-and-gown night
you embark on a trek.
It's a purpose (and God) driven life.
Let the Lord lead the way
as you travel love's path
as a newlywed husband and wife.
When the tux's been returned
and the gown's stored away
and the stresses of life hem you in,
emotions may fool you,
your passions may fade,
but love that's a choice
will not end.

This Thing Called Love

This thing called love's not hearts and doves.
It's struggle, sweat and grime.
It's hanging tough when life gets rough.
And so I wrote this rhyme.

I'll say it slow. I hope you know.
This is no average day.
This is the time for love to shine
and so my friends I pray

that you will find the means to mine
the gold that's buried deep.
You've got to dig. You can't renege.
That's how your vows you'll keep.

For we're inclined to clutch what's mine
and seek what's best for me.
But love that lives won't take, but gives
like Christ on Calvary.

For in this life a man and wife
can see that joy and pain
each play a part to win the heart.
And so make this your aim...

Be quick to say, "I sought my way.
I'm sorry. Please forgive."
With each new dawn, let tiffs be gone.
Show grace in how you live.

And if it seems you've lost your dreams,
ask God to give you more.
To aim for goals will fuel your souls
to reach for what's in store.

And when there's pain, don't try to blame
each other for the cause.
Just recognize that life breeds sighs,
discouragement and blahs.

But in those times when lines don't rhyme
and you're reduced to tears,
Confess your cares to God in prayer.
Acknowledge that He's near.

So here you stand. Please understand.
These words aren't just for you.
They're for us all so we'll recall
what makes true love stay true.

A Fleet of Four Ships

A relation*ship* of commitment
and a companion*ship* of love
require the steward*ship* of grace
for a promised friend*ship* to last forever.

This fleet of four ships will escort
any marriage that sets sail aimed at
successfully navigating uncharted waters
and the inevitable stormy seas.

That simple fleet of four ships
will guarantee safe passage
to the desired port of
"till death us do part."

About the Wedding Prayer

When you stood there at the altar
and the pastor said, "Let's pray!"
he was asking God to help you
keep the vows you pledged that day.

He was calling on the Lord of love
to rid you of your pride.
That's what it takes to make love last
as bridegroom and as bride.

He prayed our Father would provide
the grace to persevere
when hardships come and goals collide
and hopes give way to fear.

He asked the One who knows you both
to teach you love's a choice
when feelings fail the romance test
and passion's lost its voice.

There's much you probably didn't hear
when he began to pray.
That's why I'm penning you this rhyme
on this your wedding day.

Slivers in a Father's Heart

When you stand beside your daughter
and you hear the Wedding March,
I am guessing you'll feel something
like a sliver in your heart.

Though you're thrilled beyond description
that your baby's now a bride,
you will have a strange sensation
like an itch deep down inside.

It's a bittersweetish splinter
that you cannot tweezer out
'cause it's wedged and twisted sideways.
It's what good grief's all about.

It's a shard that's caused by memories
of those precious years you had
planting seeds of faith and wisdom
as her mentor, as her dad.

It's a sliver that you'll live with.
You'll thank God that it is there,
for it's just one more reminder
what you've shared is really rare.

From the Pastor to the Prince

Prince _____, on this royal day
I think you know the drill.
Your princess waits with baited breath
to hear you say "I will."

The vows you've framed within your head
form on your nervous lips.
And seeing _____ at your side,
your heartbeat starts to skip.

Now take her hands and with your eyes
embrace her with your gaze.
Convey the joy you feel inside
on this your "day of days."

And as your reign of love begins,
let Jesus be your guide.
He laid aside His kingly rights
to serve His earthly Bride.

Your scepter is the servant's towel.
Your robe is humbleness.
If these, Prince _____, crown your love,
your marriage God will bless.

I wrote the above in anticipation of the wedding of a good friend named Philip. It was written to be read by the officiating minister just prior to the vows. Even though my friend's name inspired me to think of a royal wedding complete with a prince named Philip, any name will work.

Marriage is Like a Round of Golf

A golf-course wedding? You are blessed.
I love the way Mom Nature's dressed.
She's all dolled up. She's looking fine.
Creation sings God's praise.

First let me share some thoughts with you
before it's time to say *I do.*
Some keys to keep your love alive
so you won't grow apart.

You have to choose to do what's best
when feelings fail the romance test
and when the magic of this day
is only photographs.

The kind of marriage you desire
won't always blaze with passion's fire.
A love that lasts will ebb and flow
like seasons in a year.

Please don't insist things be your way.
By giving in, you'll win the day.
Denying self is not in vogue
but kindles dying flames.

You've got to have a common goal.
Hey! Every golf green has a hole.
A target that defines your aim
and quantifies success.

To play the fairway to the pin,
you have to have the drive to win.
There're hazards and rough spots ahead
(and no avoiding them).

You also have to overlook
each other's faults. That's in God's book.
Amazing concept known as grace
that says "I hold no grudge."

Be quick to say, "I just don't know."
That's how we learn. That's how we grow.
It's how we practice honesty.
There's strength in being weak.

Replace your divots. Holler "fore!"
Don't be consumed with keeping score.
Instead, enjoy the chance to play
while walking side-by-side.

To finish strong you'll need a friend
who knows the course from start to end.
I know a caddy who will do.
He knows this game by heart.

Let God the Father walk with you
until your final hole is through.
He'll guide and help you all the way
if you but seek Him out.

** Outdoor weddings at golf courses are common in the Pacific
Northwest where I live. This was written for one such occasion.*

Time for a Marriage Tune-up

When your idle really doesn't
and your engine starts to ping,
when your spark plugs fail to fire,
you're in trouble. Here's the thing…

I'm not talking bout your Honda.
It's your marriage that I mean.
Like a car, it needs a tune up
to fulfill your wedding dreams.

On the road trip called love's journey,
flats can happen. Even worse,
radiators lose their coolant.
So remember this wee verse…

Don't ignore those routine tune-ups.
What is prized must be maintained.
Weekly dates with honest talking
will result in mileage gained.

FUNERALS

A Time to Grieve

A prayer for those who have miscarried.

A source of joy, a longed-for life
(conceived in love's embrace),
for reasons known alone to God,
took flight for Heaven today.

Without warning, without permission,
an anticipated newborn's cry
gave way to a couple's tears.

Some call it miscarriage,
a misnomer at best.
There was never more care given
to this tiny one carried within.
Carried with confidence.
Carried with pride.
And carried with a sense of the mystery of God.

And now, precious Father,
please carry my friends
in Your sturdy enveloping arms.
Carry them gently. Carry them well.
Carry them safely through their pain.
Please give them the words to express
their seemingly indescribable and inevitable grief.
And when their sorrow is spent,
please dry their eyes.

Reflections on a Still-Birth

Still-born, but, nonetheless,
you were still born.
You left us before we knew
what was happening to you.
And we didn't have a clue
we'd feel such loss.
Through the holy passage
called birth,
you were graced with a name
and a place in history.
It is plain to see,
you were an image
of your mommy and of me.
And we loved you, precious child.
How dearly we loved you.
And we will honor your memory
with a place in our hearts.
And we will speak your name
as one who lived.
For you did for a time
in a secret (and very sacred) place.
God alone knows
why you were still-born.
But, you were nonetheless, still born.

*I penned this poem for a young couple in my congregation in
Illinois who were struggling to verbalize their unexpressed
sorrow when their baby was born dead.*

Memories

Happy times.
Hard times.
Precious times.
Memories.
Before she left for heaven,
your mother left you a lifetime of memories.
Moments frozen in time
that will warm your heart
on those cold lonely nights yet to come.
Memories.

A family album of Kodak smiles
and unmistakable glances.
Snapshots of a remarkable wife,
mother, grandmother and friend,
who loved life intensely
and cherished those with whom she shared it.
A woman who walked with God
and tasted grace and taught you
it hurts to choose wrong.
Though weak in recent weeks,
your mother's faith was strong.
Memories.

They're like songs in the night
that soothe the soul,
serenading the grief-struck to sleep.
Memories.

They're for keeps.
No one can take them from you.
And whereas heartache and sorrow
will eventually fade away, memories never will.
Like the eternal life your mom now claims,
they're a gift.
Cherish them well.

The Trip of a Lifetime

He took a trip the other day.
You waved and he was gone.
And though the night closed in on you,
he glimpsed a joyful dawn.

He left the baggage of his life
most gratefully behind.
No longer weak, infirmed or pale,
no longer frail and blind.

Your loved one's luggage had been packed
for years before that day.
He had his ticket safe in hand.
His journey had been paid.

It was a trip he'd longed to take.
He'd dreamed of it for years.
The purpose for which we've been born
that wipes away our tears.

So when he heard a voice call out,
"For Heaven? All aboard!"
He bounded up the golden steps
to meet his precious Lord.

The Halls of Heaven

The halls of heaven bustle with the faithful,
who persevered until their race was won.
At home at last, they long for us to follow.
They wait and watch as we continue on
to reach the joy of that Eternal City

and hear the Father's voice say, "Child, well done!"
The choice is ours to finish what we started,
to keep the promises we made in love,
to hurdle over obstacles life sends us,
to turn a cheek when others push and shove,
to go the distance when our wills are weary,
to run our race aware of those above.

So let us run with Christ as our example,
not giving up when pressures pull us down,
looking beyond our present-day afflictions
to glimpse a goal... a priceless victor's crown.
God give us grace to reach our destination
with head held high, our hopes to fin'lly own.

(tune: Finlandia)

The Day You Died

The day for which you long had dreamed
was marked by wonder. So it seemed.
I met your family in your room
prepared to say goodbye.

We gathered round you as you slept
and sang your favorite hymns... and wept.
It was a very sacred time.
We sensed you'd soon be gone.

I traced the cross upon your brow.
I kissed your cheek and then I bowed
to pray God's blessing on your soul
and thank the Lord for you.

As you, dear brother, breathed your last,
my thoughts went back to times since past
when we would share our memories
and praise God's faithfulness.

The Kiss of Death

When you kiss a slab of granite
in a grassy field of stones,
warm lips aren't there
as once they were,
returning your embrace.
What you feel is the icy chill
of what has taken place.
With the sting of sudden loss,
it slaps you in the face.
Bent low by grief,
you give lip service
to what you were taught
as a child to be true.
And before your pilgrimage
of pain is through,
I pray you'll reach with hope to God
and find His waiting arms.

An Alzheimer's Victim's Reward

Emancipation.
Dad is free at last.
His slavery's past.
His confinement
in a confusing corridor
that wound through
his brilliant mind,
leaving him feeling lost,
is but a memory only.

Destination.
Dad is finally home.
He's not alone.
His lifelong journey
that included
breathtaking vistas
and heartbreaking valleys
has come to an end.

Celebration.
Dad is now complete
at Jesus' feet.
His marathon run
that demanded
all he could muster
was not an exercise in vain.
It resulted in
a grace-filled reward.

Yes, Dad was emancipated
that he might reach his destination.
And thus we celebrate life.
This one.

But even more,
the one to come.

In this park marked by cold headstones
and windblown stick trees,
we are warmed by this reality.

The bare branches will soon blossom.
A kiss from the rising Son
will awaken the dark dormant earth
from its long winter sleep.
Spring is coming.
Of that we can be sure.

Butterfly Faith

A fuzzy worm (in time) becomes
a silk-winged butterfly.
And that describes so beautifully
what happens when we die.

No longer earthbound, we can soar.
At last, we're fully free.
The old is gone. The new has come.
The best is yet to be.

A Leaf That Fell Too Soon

Alive to life... and sensitive.
A gentle man. A leaf.
A leaf whose fall was premature.
His autumn colors brief.

A textured leaf. Complex and bright.
Deprived of symmetry.
A leaf that weathered winter's chill
but came at last to see

that love's pure joys are rarely found
in pleasures that we seek.
They're found instead denying self
when trials leave us weak.

And in his weakness, he found strength
to give his faith away.
The Son shone through this fragile leaf
in what our friend would say.

We'll not forget this one we loved.
God's Book will press this leaf.
And to God's Book we look for hope
to guide us in our grief.

** I had a cousin who lived much of his adult life in the gay
community. Because of his inability to reconcile his lifestyle
with his Evangelical roots, he abused drugs and alcohol. A
dozen years before his death, he returned to his childhood faith
with a repentant heart and much joy. By God's grace, he lived
a celibate life. I wrote this poem for his memorial service.*

Reflections on Interment

What we deposit in a vault
or bury in the ground
are not the ones
we've known and loved.
That's not where they are found.

Their souls departed when they died.
With Christ they live in peace,
deprived of grief
that weighs us down.
From earth they've been released.

A Grief Observed

They stumble to a fresh grave.
Their unabated tears fall to the ground.
They weep in silence not knowing what to say.
One loved so deeply is dead so needlessly
(or so it seems).

Jagged shards of pain puncture places in the heart
that only days before pulsated with laughter and love.
And though the shock of what took place
has given way to the dull ache of reality,
like bullies in a darkened alley, these villains of the soul
pounce unexpectedly, blindsiding the unsuspecting
with merciless sorrow.

Stunned and hopeless, they deposit their flowers
and the fragrance of their grief and turn to leave.
There is no reason to linger any longer.
Life goes on even after life goes off.
But wait...

A voice like a penetrating sunbeam
breaks through the mist of mourning.
"Why seek the living among the dead?
The one for whom you seek is not here.
He lives."

And with that they retrace their steps
through a valley of shadows
into a shaft of light.

** This poem was written for a young mother in our church
whose Coast Guard husband was killed in a helicopter crash.
As I contemplated her grief, being left alone with an 18-month-
old daughter, I pictured the agony of the women who
approached Jesus' tomb.*

A Wardrobe in Disguise

"It won't be long now,"
you said with a smile,
your emotions under control.
And I marveled at your calm.
But when you got that call that said
all had been done
(and all was not enough),
didn't it take awhile for your ready smile
to find your face again?

You never are quite ready
for the end to come, are you?
Even when you've had wind of the end
for awhile.

When you finally face that familiar face
inside that greedy box, your resignation
to what you thought you were prepared for
quickly bolts out the door,
leaving you alone with the lonely truth
that life will never, ever, really be the same.

But as Paul Harvey was wont to say...
And now for the rest of the story!

Death's only glory is that overpriced coffin
in which he thinks he's sealed our fate
(and that of those we loved).
But Death forgets his box is but a wardrobe
through which the Risen Lion leads us
(and all those with faith)
into the Land of Narnia,
where death
(even if it could be remembered)
would be only a bad dream.

Long live Aslan!
Deep be Your peace!

Remembering Columbine

In a not-so-little town
on the front range of the Rockies,
a room designed for learning
became a tomb for those gunned down.
There were bullets and blood
and a reign of terror
followed by a flood of fear.
Wearing black trench coats
to hide their insecurities,
two boys in men's bodies
lived out the violence
they'd previously caged in their minds.
It's a nightmare that has left us
blind with rage and grief.
And for those who've lost loved ones,
there is no relief.

It's the kind of tragedy we never dreamed
would strike in our own backyard.
It's hard to explain how and why,
but we try 'cause we must,
while we simply trust
that a loving God is weeping with us
and remains in complete control.
When bullets fly, children die.
And when hearts break, we feel the ache
and reach out to those left alone,
trusting alone in God's Word.
Words that promise
that no one needs to grieve without hope.
Though the slope of life remains slippery,
we are offered stable footing
as we stand at the foot of a bloodied cross
and peer into an empty grave.

* I wrote this to honor the memory of the students who were gunned down at Columbine High School on April 20, 1999. A framed version of this poem hangs in the Visitor Center at the headquarters of Focus on the Family in Colorado Springs.

Winter's Gone, But Spring is Coming

Why's answers to a senseless tragedy in Maryville.

Mary's Son
weeps with the grief-struck
who in Maryville
ask why
should a much-loved pastor perish.
Why did
Pastor Winters die?

SPECIAL DAYS

Why a gunman?
Why on Sunday?
Why would God allow
this crime?
For what purpose
was Fred taken?
What's the reason
for this rhyme?

Even as we wait
for answers,
(even as we
question God),
we are forced to
look down deeper
than six feet
beneath the sod.

Winter's gone
but Spring is coming.
Easter's tulips
trumpet hope.
While the bagpipes
drone in sorrow,
God's Word gives us
cause to cope.

Death's defeated.
Christ is risen!
The grave has lost
its painful sting.

Bulbs once buried,
soon will flower.
In our sorrow
we can sing....

"Because He lives, I can face tomorrow..."

* *I wrote this in response to the 2009 tragedy in Maryville,
Illinois in which Pastor Fred Winters was gunned down by a
deranged gunman while preaching to his congregation on a
Sunday morning.*

DEDICATION OF A HOME

A Home Blessing

Lord, bless this place that, by Your grace,
this family now calls home.
Please fill it with all that is good and necessary.
Food and drink. Clothing and furnishings.
Art and music. Memories and dreams.
Laughter and love. Health and peace.
Please protect it from theft and fire,
as well as earthquake and flood.
Through the clouds
of sorrow and uncertainty,
would You shine Your rays
of comfort and hope?
And, Lord, may the road that leads to this home
be free from relational potholes and debris.
Let it be an unobstructed path
for those You send
to enrich each one who lives here.
And may the open door of this sanctuary
symbolize their open hearts that long to care
for all who step inside.

HOLIDAYS

A New Year Dawns

A new year dawns
and with it light to see
a new horizon
of what's yet to be.
Redemption of
my flawed humanity.
Al-le-lu-ia. Al-le-lu-ia.

A new year grants
permission to be brave
as I move on from
stress's greedy grave.
From buried dreams
and littered paths unpaved
Al-le-lu-ia. Al-le-lu-ia.

A new year means
the chance to start again,
to grant forgiveness
and to make amends.

To risk departing
from what's always been.
Al-le-lu-ia. Al-le-lu-ia.

A new year now
invites me to look up
and drink new wine
from faith's most ancient cup.
I'll toast the One
whose grace is quite enough.
Al-le-lu-ia. Al-le-lu-ia.

(tune: For All the Saints)

A Tale of Two Birds

Two cardinals resting on their perch
remind me of what's taught in church.
The old has gone. The new has come.
St. Paul called it "good news."

The brown bird now makes room for red,
as doubt gives way to hope instead.
A year of challenge, joy and loss,
succumbs to one that's new.

And while the future is unknown,
we will not face it all alone.
The truth of Christmas promises
God's with us through the year.

New Year's Dance-a-thon

As we embrace this brand new year,
we'll learn to dance with change,
as God our Father takes the lead
with moves that may seem strange.
And still the music calls to mind
that change need not be feared,
for He who knows what lies ahead
has promised to be near.

So let us waltz in gratitude
for all the Lord provides.
Our daily bread, employment too,
and loved ones by our side.
Come join the new year's dance-a-thon
with twists and turns and spins.
Let's find our feet, kick up our heels
and leave the lead to Him.

(tune: Auld Lang Syne)

A New Year's Prayer

While resolutions weary me,
I still have one resolve.
To live each day for You alone,
as weeks and months evolve.

The challenges this year will bring
will drop me to my knees.
And so I'm asking You, dear Lord,
to give me wisdom. Please!

Direct my steps along a path
that isn't always clear.
And when I'm forced to make a choice,
don't let me cave to fear.

I hope this year will prove my trust
in what You've planned for me.
So give me grace, dear loving God,
to live expectantly.

SANCTITY-OF-LIFE SUNDAY

Her Guilt's Like Acid Rain

Lord Jesus, be near my hurting friend.
Her eyes speak the pain that she bears.
She aches in her heart from a heartless mistake
she made when she was young.

It seemed so right then.
But then was when her only concern was a choice.
And left to her choice and society's voice,
what she thought was right proved all wrong.

And though that happened years ago,
before she called You Lord,
the guilt of her past (like acid rain)
still burns inside her soul.

I know You have cried for her sorrow.
Please release her from kidnapping fear.
Would you help her to know she one day will hold
the child she longs to be near?

A Choice to Make

Being pro-life has to do with more than just unborn babies.

There's a choice that we are given
every day we live our lives.
Will we disregard the helpless
or make sure they will survive?

Those at risk hide in the shadows,
robbed of justice with no voice.
Will we speak up for these victims?
That's the question. That's our choice.

In a womb or in an alley,
in South Asia or Iraq,
there are victims close to dying
who need more than Christian talk.

They are persons in God's image
and as humans, they should live.
They cry out for liberation,
but they're silenced lest we give

of our time (our precious hours),
of our wealth (we all are rich),
of our heart's preoccupation
(being done with envy's itch).

We've been called as liberators
to release the overlooked.
It's a mission we've been given,
specified in God's own book.

But this question begs an answer.
Is our willingness a ruse?
Or will we prove our intentions
by our actions? We must choose.

Life is Precious

Life is precious, sacred, blest
from the womb to final rest.
God is in a child's first breath
and a grandpa facing death.

Special-needs autistic son.
Crippled daughter who can't run.
Those impaired in speech or sight.
Those whose hearing isn't right.

Those who can't recall their name.
Those with damage to their brain.
Those in prison, addicts too.
Those who think their options few.

Each life matters. Each has worth.
Everyone on "God's green earth."
Life is precious, sacred, blest
from the womb to final rest.

I Will Be

I will be a voice of justice
on behalf of the unborn,
speaking out for helpless children
still in process, being formed.
I will sing the praise of Yahweh
who conceives what they'll become
when they've grown to their adulthood,
someone's daughter, someone's son.

I will be a sanctuary
to those bruised by acts of hate
who are victims of dysfunction,
feeling they've been doomed by Fate.

I will shelter them from danger.
I will seek to shield their pain.
By God's grace I'll offer healing
so their wounds won't be in vain.

I will be a port of refuge
to the dying rocked by fear.
In their eyes I'll see God's image
when their thinking's rarely clear.
Celebrating life as precious,
I will offer dignity
and reach out as though to Jesus,
until death has set them free.

I will be a means God uses
to declare the gift of life
in the sanctity of marriage
of a husband and a wife.
In the realm of all things living,
breeds and species of the earth,
I will celebrate creation
with its priceless, holy worth.

A Grazing Mace

A grazing mace can caught my eye.
I'm blind but now can see.
The wretch who threw it at my face
hates protestors like me.

I demonstrate for human rights,
including unborn kids.
My protest signs display God's love
for those abused and hid.

Through dingy mangers soiled by terror,
too many women come
to leave behind a fetal mass...
a lifeless human one.

Amazingly, God gives me grace
to love those who deny
the rights of those as yet unborn,
who will most likely die.

Though scarred by fleshing out my faith,
my blinded eyes still hold
a vision for the world God planned.
I'll picket till I'm old.

(tune: Amazing Grace)

God's Masterpiece

With palette, paint and brush in hand,
the Artist has at His command
the simple tools by which He will
create a masterpiece.

But at the start you'd never know
what one day will be best-of-show
is nothing more than colored globs
that seem like a mistake.

"Forget it!" one voice quickly cries.
"Don't waste your time!" another sighs.
"There's just no way that what He's done
will ever be acclaimed."

HOLIDAYS

The Artist hears, but doesn't turn.
He knows that some who scoff might learn
that what they see as random strokes
is priceless art indeed.

But from the start there is no way
to tell what will emerge one day,
and so the Artist's infant work
is often mocked and tossed.

And when it is the Artist grieves,
for what in love His mind conceived
will never be the work of art
He knew would bless a home.

And all because uncultured folks,
who thought His masterpiece a joke,
are free to wreck what is not theirs
and judge the Artist wrong.

Is that the freedom wars have won?
Where works of art are left undone
because it's thought until they're framed
they're free to be destroyed?

May God forbid! May He paint on
without the claims that He is wrong.
For every life's a masterpiece
the moment He begins.

MARTIN LUTHER KING DAY

God Has a Dream, Too!

Martin Luther King wasn't the only dreamer.

Selma, Memphis, Birmingham,
Atlanta and D.C.
These cities are synonymous
with dreams God has for me.

To take a stand for those who can't.
To be an advocate
for those oppressed by prejudice
and victims of neglect.

God hopes that I will serve the poor,
the widows and bereaved.
That I will be the arms of Christ
to anyone in need.

The message preached by Martin King
(like Matthew, Luke and John)
is what God dreams will mark my life
till what He hates is gone.

Remembering a King and a President

This week we honored Martin King
recalling how he served
the poor, deprived and dispossessed,
denied what they deserved.
We're grateful, Lord, for patriots
who stand for what You will,
who dare to do whate'er it takes
to conquer culture's ills.

And, Lord, we're mindful of the fact
we've still a ways to go.
In four decades since Martin's death,
our progress has been slow.

Please guide us, God, and bless our land
in spite of all its flaws.
Please lead our sitting President
and those who make our laws.

(tune: America the Beautiful)

Prince of Peace

In the year the market fell,
well...

A king had a son
who'd be known as
a prince of peace
in a world of hate.

He was named after
a pastor in Germany
who has branded an enemy
over the stand he took,
understood by a few.

His name was a clue
that his life
(also lived as a pastor)
would be played in a minor key.

Still, Martin Luther King
taught us how to sing
the lyrics of love.

In 1968
hate stilled his voice
but not his song.

It is still heard
in schools and churches
and city squares and everywhere
the color of a person's blood
matters more than
the color of their skin.

Peace be to his memory
and to the world he Nobel-y served.

PRESIDENTS' DAY

A Post-Inaugural Prayer

This Tuesday past, a President
was sworn in once again.
Most gracious God, we intercede
for Michelle and for him.

With his two hands he voiced his vows.
He raised his right hand high.
But with his left, he palmed a Book
that answers every why.

Allow that Book to be his guide
throughout the next four years.
In spite of those who will object,
help him deflect their jeers.

With solemn swear, he sought Thy help
while we watched on TV.
Lord, let him sense Thy presence near
whenever he seeks Thee.

Preserve him, Lord. Protect his heart.
Defend him from attacks
as he stands up for truth and life
and brings old values back.

A Prayer for Our Commander-in-Chief

The world weighs heavy on his heart
as hopes for peace are blown apart
and facts concealed for safety's sake
are leaked like toxic waste.

His brow betrays the stress he bears.
So, too, the gray that gilds his hair.
That's why we're called to intercede
for one the critics taunt.

Our President is being squeezed
so we must drop down to our knees
and ask the Lord to give him strength
for pressures he must face.

Give him the judgment that he needs
and lift the burden as he leads.
O, God, please gird our President
with tempered-steel resolve.

A Prayer that Pleases God

Our God is pleased when on our knees
we lift our President
and intercede for him who leads
our nation's government.

It's good to pray and humbly say
how grateful we all are
because this man who guides our land
has learned from failure's scars.

Perhaps he knows that like a rose
God finds prayer's fragrance sweet.
At any rate, he thinks it's great
we pray for him each week.

A Prayer for the First Father

As he lays them down to sleep,
our nation's shepherd tends his sheep.
He says a prayer within his heart.
for both his little girls.

And as he sits beside their beds,
he contemplates their joys and dread.
He senses what they can't express
that pulsates in their hearts.

This one we call our President
believes his girls are heaven-sent
and that he has a special role
no other man can play.

So, Father, please be near this dad
who hugs his lambs when they are sad
and sings their praises with much pride
when they achieve at school.

As the father of three daughters, I wrote this for President Obama and his two girls. Mr. Obama was elected the day my dad's election as a child of God was certified (November 4, 2008).

God, Please Guide Our President

Almighty God,
lest the man in the White House
become prematurely gray,
would You ease the burden
he daily shoulders
on behalf of our whole country?
That he might lead us with confidence,
won't You gift him with wisdom
that comes only from You?
That he might serve us with humility,
won't You lift him on the wings of prayer
into Your very presence?
That he might remain a man of integrity,
won't You sift his motives
so that what is pure
would rise above what isn't?
That he might pursue Your plan
instead of his hunches,
make him willing to shift his direction
when a change in course is necessary.
As he closes his eyes in prayer each day,
please open his heart to what You'd say
and fill him with the strength he needs
to follow where You lead. Amen.

ST. PATRICK'S DAY

I'm Looking Over a Three-Leaf Clover

New lyrics celebrating an old saint's ingenuity.

I'm looking over
a three-leaf clover
that Saint Patrick saw before.
One leaf's the Father.
The second's the Son.
Third is the Spirit.
There're three yet there's one.
It takes explaining
'cause faith is waning.
There's absence of mystery.

In Dublin or Dover,
St. Paddy's clover
can teach us the Trinity.
St. Pat the preacher
was one grand teacher
to illustrate truth through weeds.

Old Mother Nature
revealed Father God.
Clovers decoded
what many found odd.
In Shamrock City
I pray this ditty
will reclaim an old saint's fame.
He was a master.
A much-loved pastor.
Let's honor St. Patrick's name.

(tune: I'm Looking Over a Four-Leaf Clover)

An Irish Table Grace

Our Father's eyes are smiling
'cause He loves the likes of we.
He's the God of all compassion
for we're selfish as can be.
The shamrock is a symbol
of a God who's one but three.
And in Patrick's name we honor
He who died for you and me.

(tune: When Irish Eyes are Smiling)

TAX DAY

A Table Grace for Tax Day

This day in April our favorite Uncle
taxes our patience and our reserves.
But when we itemize all our blessings,
we can't deny him what he deserves.

With all our cousins throughout the country,
we pass our Uncle's star-spangled hat.
This is an offering funding our freedom
envied in Cuba and in Iraq.

So on this Tax Day, we sing his praises
thanking our Father for Uncle Sam.
Even in lean times, we are most wealthy.
Nieces and nephews... A-mer-icans.

(tune: Morning Has Broken)

EARTH DAY

Earth Day Anthem

O, God, forbid that smoggy skies
should choke the whooping crane.
May our misuse of fossil fuels
give way to fields of grain.
May green become as popular
as are red, white and blue.
Let the resources we enjoy
be those that can renew.

America the Beautiful.
May those three words again
be sung in schools and county fairs
and baseball stadiums.
But first let beauty be restored
by keeping roadways clean
as we put litter in its place
and through recycling.

(Tune: America the Beautiful)

Mother Nature's Death Wish

This very week Earth Day draws near.
Most eerily it's very clear
how sick our planet seems to be.
Just ponder what has been.

The Waco cult Davidian
revealed the human heart of sin
as senseless killings stunned us all
and soaked the ground with blood.

Fast-forward then another year
when Oklahomans shed their tears
for victims of a downtown bomb
who died so needlessly.

It was this week in Ninety-nine
we gasped to learn of Columbine
as Littleton became big news
we wished we'd never heard.

And now this week Virginia Tech
has left us all a nervous wreck.
Ironically, though tulips bloom,
our spring has lost its step.

NATIONAL DAY OF PRAYER

A National Call to Prayer

Americans, let's pause today
to seek the Lord and humbly pray.
Let's ask that those who lead our land
will heed His truth and take a stand.

But first of all let's bend our knees
and ask the Lord for what He sees.
With honest gaze let's look within
for motives that give way to sin.

Let's own our culpability,
confessing what we've failed to be,
then listen for what God might say
in judgment of the U.S.A.

Let's beg His mercy and His grace
for godless norms, perverse and base.
Let's pledge to push for purity
while guarding others' dignity.

Let's ask for eyes to see the poor
and hearts that ache for troops at war.
Let's plead for justice on behalf
of those whose plight makes bullies laugh.

Let's bow our heads and fold our hands
and ask the Lord to heal our land.

In God We Trust

Just like our dollars say,
In God We Trust today
for what we need.
Food for our appetite,
homes where we sleep at night
and laws to help us know what's right
in word and deed.

We love this God-blessed land
where freedom takes a stand
on war-torn feet.
May we acknowledge Him,
bending our knees again
and turning from our willful sin
God's ways to greet.

(tune: My Country 'Tis of Thee)

A Call to Prayer

A pensive Abe sits on his throne,
With open eyes he prays alone.
He looks toward a marble house
beyond a grassy mall.

From Lincoln's shrine we take our cues
and not the headlines of the news.
We pause to seek God's purposes
for this great land we love.

We set aside a day for prayer
when, in a well-worn winged-back chair,
we ask the Lord to help us know
for whom to cast our vote.

Lord, give us flint-like faith to face
the questions that we will embrace
within this long election stretch
when flip answers fall short.

Praying for Our Leaders

Lord, help our leaders keep their vows
when lust would have them take a bow
and stoop to infidelity.
Please help them to be strong.

Lord, govern those who govern us.
Inspire them to keep our trust.
Encourage them to stand upright.
Please help them shun what's wrong.

Lord, guide the ones who make our laws.
In spite of ego, guilt and flaws,
attune their ears to hear Your voice.
Please help them serve Your will.

Praying With Liberty

With Liberty we lift our hands,
beseeching God to bless our land
and guide our leaders to a place
where righteousness prevails.

With Liberty we stand erect,
although ashamed and circumspect
about the countless times we've failed
to stand for what is right.

With Liberty we raise a flame,
confessing that we are to blame
for how we've bowed to tolerance
and closed our eyes to truth.

With Liberty we dodge the tide
that splashes us from side to side
and keep our heads above the fray
that harbors culture's lies.

With Liberty we clutch a book
without concern for how we look
when critics see us with God's Word
and simply roll their eyes.

With Liberty we lift our eyes
and look into the spacious skies
to seek God's vision and His peace
and focus on His grace.

For Kings and Queens and Presidents

St. Paul reminds us we should pray
for those in government.
For those God wills to lead our land,
for kings and presidents.

St. Paul reminds us to press on.
To look (with hope) ahead.
To not be anxious or complain,
but seek the Lord instead.

St. Paul reminds us we are called
to voice what we believe.
To stand up for the little guy
and widows left to grieve.

Where in the World Is God?

While millions wonder
where Matt Lauer's broadcasting today,
I'd dare say several million more
are asking as they pray...

"Where in the world are You, my God?
Have you forsaken me?
I feel abandoned, lost, alone,
adrift on some dark sea.

"It feels as though You're deaf to prayers
I've launched from hopeful lips.
My anguished heart is overwhelmed.
My faith has lost its grip.

"The calendar reminds me
that today's the Day of Prayer.
But frankly, Lord, I cannot pray.
It seems that You don't care.

"And so, dear Lord, for these who think
You're anywhere but near,
I'm asking that You offer clues
that indicate You're here.

"Break through the fog and help them know
(in spite of how they feel)
that You hear every prayer they pray
and have the power to heal.

"That You, though sometimes silent,
have a plan You're working out.
A plan that's not upended
when our trust gives way to doubt."

A Prayer for Lawmakers (and Me)

Guide those who govern us, O God.
Enable them to weave into the fabric of our society
threads of morality and truth that will not fray.
And as I legislate the choices
that dictate the way I behave each day,
may I do so mindful of Your law of love
that is more concerned with spirit than letter.

Help me guard each person's dignity
and protect their human rights,
even when they choose a way of life
or embrace a belief that I believe
is less than You desire.
Give me the willingness, courage and patience
to embody the grace of Your gospel,
accepting those I meet with unconditional love,
all the while convinced
that You are already at work in their lives.

God Remains

An anthem for a fearful nation.

God remains our source of courage
when we're traumatized by fear.
When we're haunted by the headlines
and the stock reports we hear.
Yet God whispers in the silence,
"Don't despair, I'm in control.
Hurting hearts and broken cities
will at last one day be whole."

God remains our source of comfort
in this bleak economy.
When predictions voiced from Wall Street
pry away our inner peace.
Still God whispers in the silence,
"When banks fail and markets fall,
I won't leave you or forsake you.
I'll sustain you through it all."

God invites us to be trusting
when we find that faith is hard.
When we're fearful for the future
and our nerves are frayed or jarred.

Hear God whisper in the silence,
"Even when your faith is weak,
I will keep your feet from stumbling,
though your way is dark and bleak."

(tune: What a Friend We Have in Jesus)

MOTHERS' DAY

A Prayer for Moms

Dear Father, mothers in our land
need daily grace to cope.
So many pine for sons at war.
They're running low on hope.

And other moms can't bear to face
what storm clouds blew away.
Tornados broke their homes and hearts.
Please comfort them we pray.

Some mothers ache for wayward kids.
Some grieve for those who've died
while others long to see their kids
develop healthy pride.

Be near the one whose son holds court
within an oval room.
Please help this mom to comfort George
when headlines foster gloom.

All mothers in our nation know
the joy of giving birth.
But, Lord, we ask you'll help each mom
to sense her in-bred worth.

With Gratitude for Mother-like Love

Our Father God, we thank You for our mothers
who cradled us when we were small and weak.
Then as we grew, they clothed us with compassion.
They coaxed first steps and coached us how to speak.
Protecting us from "monsters in our closets,"
they sang us lullabies to help us sleep.

Our Father God, we thank You for our mothers
who cooked our meals and baked our birthday cakes.
Who read us stories, helped us with our homework,
becoming nurses when our bodies ached.
They put our wants before the things they needed,
consoling us when lovesick hearts would break.

Our Father God, You are just like a mother.
With caring arms you slake our thirst for love.
You pick us up when failures leave us fallen.
You hold us close when bullies push and shove.
You wipe away the tears that stain our faces.
You are the perfect parent we dream of.

Our Father God, there is no other mother
who can compare with all the love You give.
Your mother's heart envelopes us as children.
Your grace and mercy give us strength to live.
With tenderness You welcome our confession,
and give assurance that You do forgive.

(tune: Finlandia)

Longing for a Birth Mother

In the womb of one I never knew,
I grew as one with her
until the day she gave me birth
and gave me up and stepped out of my life
for the rest of hers.
But now as I reach the autumn of my years,
shelved emotions of forbidden questions begin to
tumble down unbidden.
Questions that can no longer be silenced.
Who am I?
Who was she?
Why was I never meant to be raised
by the one who first called me her child?
Why do I care more
than I ever thought I possibly could?
Would it all best be left undone?
Do I look more like my father or my mother?
Did either of them ever think of what became of me?
The questions, Lord, keep coming.
And as I turn to face them,
please help me embrace them without fear.
Remind me that because I call you Father,
my worth is ultimately in You.

** I wrote this on behalf of friends and family members who were
adopted, including my father-in-law and my brother's two
children.*

Longing for Mother's Nest

When you are given up at birth,
in time you come to doubt your worth.
You feel rejected, bruised inside.
A wound that never heals.

If you're adopted there's a hole
that permeates your very soul.
And though you're raised by loving folks,
you long for something more.

That's just the way it is, I guess,
for those removed from mother's nest.
You learn to fly, but fail to soar
and can't explain quite why.

A Day to Remember

It was a day you think of often.
When your mom said "Can we chat?"
when she pulled out faded photos
while you asked her "Who is that?"

It was a day that you discovered
that the one who gave you birth
also gave you what she couldn't.
A chance to thrive. A sense of worth.

It was a day emotions bubbled
like a pot of boiling stew.
Being told what had been secret,
made you wonder what was true?

It was a day you felt rejected,
silenced by what you had heard.
Ill equipped to share your feelings.
Wanting to be reassured.

It was a day you heard God whisper,
"You were chosen to be loved.
Though adopted, you're most special.
I have plans you know not of."

It was a day you hugged your parents
smiling through a veil of tears,
praising them for what they gave you
through a childhood of years.

MEMORIAL DAY

Memorial Day Ponderings

Come Monday, we will pause to think
about a chain formed link by link
that binds us to the liberties
that God desires for all.

It is a day for looking back
at how the mourners' dreaded black
maintains the colors that we love...
the red, the white and blue.

In cemeteries far and near,
small flags at grave sites make it clear
that freedom's price was freely paid
by those who spent their lives.

And so on this Memorial Day,
we place a wreath and humbly pray
that these who died courageously
will not have died in vain.

A Grave Reminder

In Arlington and Gettysburg
and graveyards of which few have heard,
those small white markers sanctify
the hallowed ground beneath.

They speak of veterans who are dead,
who overcame their sense of dread
to undermine the enemy
and prepay what we own.
What we now claim was purchased then
by soldiers who would fight again
to guarantee our cherished rights,
which makes our country great.

Each tiny marker boasts the name
of one who never savored fame
but served his Uncle selflessly,
not needing to be known.

We thank You, God, for these now gone
and for their memories that live on.
As we place wreaths and flags in love,
grace us with healthy pride.

Don't Take Memorial Day for Granted

They called it Decoration Day,
a chance each year to humbly say
how much we owe to those now gone
who blazed our freedom trail.

It is a day to leave our homes
and journey to a yard of bones
where those who served sleep six feet down,
awaiting Gabriel's horn.

It's there we'll place a plant or wreath
and think of those who lay beneath.
We'll thank the Lord for what they did
to benefit our lives.

In cemeteries far and near,
we'll say a prayer and shed a tear
and count the cost of liberty
they paid on our behalf.

We'll also grieve for moms and dads,
recalling special times we had.
And we'll resolve to spend less time
at work and more at home.

It is a somber holiday
which calls for more than rest and play.
It is for taking stock
of bonds that made us rich.

FATHERS' DAY

A Fathers' Day Wish

I wish for you a life that's marked
by laughter, joy and love.
A life that corresponds to what
you've long been dreaming of.

I wish for you a thirst for God
that won't be ever slaked.
May hungering for what He wants,
guide every choice you make.

I wish for you both roots and wings
when it comes time to leave.
Take pride in who your family is,
but go... explore... achieve.

I wish for you the kind of job
that prompts your heart to sing.
Where what you do (not what you make)
is really everything.

I wish for you contentment, too.
Don't strive for just more stuff.
Learn how to say "I could, but won't"
and when to say "Enough!"

I wish for you (if God should will)
a mate who's your best friend.
A partner who will keep love's vows
until through death they end.

I wish for you (if God permits)
the chance to parent kids.
For in that role you'll understand
the whys in what I did.

I wish you opportunities
to learn another's plight,
so that you're less inclined to judge
a view you think's not right.

I wish for you sufficient pain
to cause your faith to grow.
You'll find in times of suffering
"I hope" becomes "I know."

I wish for you a grateful heart
aware of your true wealth.
The greatest riches in the world
are family, friends and health.

I wish for you the means to say
"I know my dad loves me."
For there could be no truer truth.
I'm proud as proud can be.

** I wrote this for my three daughters as they stood at the
threshold of a new season of life; leaving home and facing the
world on their own.*

When You Lose Your Dad

A Father to the fatherless.
God loves to play that role
when death has robbed you of your dad
and grief invades your soul.

He carries you in arms of love
and whispers in your ear
that time will heal your broken heart
and wipe away your tears.

So let the Father father you.
Admit you're just a child
who needs to grieve and long for one
whose memories make you smile.

A Prayer of Thanks for My Dad

Lord, I thank You for my father,
who (with Mother) gave me life.
He was stressed by grueling hardships,
yet not sidelined by his strife.
Persevering without quitting.
Hero status since my youth.
He cared much about my future,
though at times he seemed aloof.

Lord, I thank You for my father.
Though imperfect, he came through.
He was strong and yet was tender,
showing me all I could do.
Tying shoes or shooting baskets,
riding bikes or skipping stones.
He helped me in times of trouble
when I called him on the phone.

Lord, I thank You for my father.
In my mind I see him there.
Wrinkled face and stooping shoulders,
calloused hands and graying hair.

Thanks for moments that You gave me
to remind him what he meant
when I tried to share my feelings
for the special times we spent.

Lord, I thank you for my father
who has crossed the finish line.
His long marathon is over,
I'm still struggling, left behind.
Solemnly I bless his memory,
grateful for his legacy.
May the "treasures" that he gave me
be the wealth my children see in me.

(tune: Glorious Things of Thee Are Spoken)

Singing My Father's Praise

When I think of my father, I see him at home
near his flat-screen TV on his black leather throne.

It's a scene that's imprinted, engraved in my head.
A portrait I'll cherish long after he's dead.

The king of our family enthroned by the fire,
who seeks Heaven's Kingdom and speaks his desire.

A monarch who studies the Scriptures each day,
embracing what God wants as he bows to pray.

From that chair he prays for his sons and their wives,
with hope that the Lord's will is first in their lives.

He prays for his grandchildren, each one by name,
concerned that the culture might snuff out faith's flame.

He sips at his coffee (one sugar, no cream)
and wonders why cancer has cut short his dreams.

And yet while reclining, he knows all too well
his reign's been a good one. That's easy to tell.

Just talk to his tenants, his neighbors and friends.
They'll honor my father with praise that won't end.

** During the final months of my dad's life, I found myself
writing several rhyming expressions that described both my
father and my love for him. This is one of them.*

A Final Birthday Wish

Today's my father's last birthday
before he passes on.
The cancer's traveled through his bones.
I know he'll soon be gone.

His face is gaunt. His body's frail.
Yet in his tired eyes
I still can see a gleam of hope
his shriveled frame denies.

He doesn't want a piece of cake.
He has no need for gifts.
Our presence is what he wants most.
That's what gives him a lift.

Surrounded by the ones he loves,
my dad flashes a smile.
That boyish grin I've cherished since
I was a chubby child.

He smiled when I learned to walk.
When I first rode a bike.
He beamed with pride to see me preach
behind a pulpit mike.

He smiled at my firstborn's birth.
He grinned when I went gray.
His knowing smile eased the pain
when our pet passed away.

Today he's 82 years old.
The age at which he'll die.
The thought of it knots up my gut.
I breathe a heavy sigh.

I also breathe a whispered prayer
of gratitude and praise.
My father's impact on my life
will last beyond his days.

** I read this to my dad on March 14, 2008. He died on
November 4 of that same year.*

FOURTH OF JULY

Independence Day Prayer

America is our Creator's canvas
on which He's painted quite a wonderland.
With awe we contemplate creation's beauty.
Five lakes called great and one deep canyon grand.
The Rocky Mountains and the windswept prairies,
Alaska's tundra and Mojave's sand.

O, God, we bow in penitential sorrow,
confessing our resistance to Your way.
We've left undone the good that was our duty
while we have done our best to disobey.
We've let our culture dictate norms and values
and dodged Truth's debt that one day we must pay.

Forgive us, Lord. We have no hope without You.
Absolve the guilt our nation has incurred.
Remove the stain of corporate transgressions.
Remind us, God, that prayers (through faith) are heard.
Restore the values that once marked our country.
Revive our souls and may our hearts be stirred.

(tune: Finlandia)

A Prayer for America the Beautiful

For spacious skies, for waves of grain,
for purple peaks and fruited plains
and godly pilgrims who first came,
we bow our heads in Jesus' name.

We thank You, God, for this great land
sustained by Your most gracious hand
and for a president who stands
for what your moral law demands.

We bow before You on this day,
confessing how we've gone astray
by turning black and white to gray
while seeking wealth and our own way.

Forgive us, Father. We have failed
to serve the homeless and those jailed
while Mother Justice wept and wailed,
as did your Son who once was nailed.

Be near our troops as they defend
the freedoms of our Arab friends.
And yet, we pray this war will end
so grieving hearts can finally mend.

Make us one nation under You,
convinced "in God we trust" is true.
Restore our hope as we renew
our pledge to pray, speak up and do.

The Symbols of Freedom

The symbols of our land abound.
A flag, a dome, a bell.
They speak of what we all hold dear.
The freedoms we know well.

And there are symbols of our faith.
A cross, a cup, some bread.
They call us to remember Him
who for true freedom bled.

So let us heed the call today
and freely celebrate
the fact that Christ died for our sin
and that our country's great.

I'm Loving Life

I love the Lord. I love His church.
I love my kids and wife.
I love my friends and where I work.
I'd say I love my life.

I'm proud to be a citizen
of this great God-blessed land.
I love the flag that we salute
and that for which it stands.

I'm grateful that my eyes can still
behold dawn's early light
and for two ears that still can hear
the song of birds in flight.

I'm thankful that my nose still smells,
that I can taste my food
and for those Gospel melodies
that lift my downcast mood.

What's not to love about my life?
I'm wealthy as can be.
Forgiven. Graced. And loved by One
whose Son has set me free.

** I wrote this especially for Bill and Gloria Gaither and their
2008 Lovin' Life Homecoming Concert Series.*

A Somber Birthday Celebration

My grandma and my uncle
share a birthday. It's today.
My father's mom died years ago,
but Sam's alive, though gray.

HOLIDAYS

I celebrate his birth each year
with fireworks and fun.
But lately I'm concerned his days on earth
may soon be done.

I fear my uncle's health is poor.
He's looking gaunt and thin.
He doesn't stand for much these days.
His plight has crippled him.

Where once he claimed to trust in God,
my uncle's waffling.
He trips a lot on tolerance.
His step has lost its spring.

His apathy's begun to spread.
He can't feel much these days.
He's blind to things that moved him once.
He's deaf to virtue's ways.

His heart is weak. It doesn't race
to see "Old Glory" fly.
His feeble hand can't reach his chest
when veterans' floats pass by.

He doesn't quite know who he is.
His memory isn't good.
He can't recall what made him great.
Oh, how I wish he could.

He's very sick. He just might die.
But Sam's a tough old bird.
I'm praying for a miracle.
Do you think that absurd?

My birthday wish for Uncle Sam
is that he will survive.
At two-hundred-and-thirty-two,
he's not too old to thrive.

** Yes, it's true. My All-American paternal grandmother,
Margaret Stradley Turley, was born on July 4, 1897 in Bland
County, Virginia. She married my grandfather, Haralambos
Asimakoupoulos, a Greek immigrant, who settled near Lapwai,
Idaho. While both my paternal grandparents are safe in the
arms of Jesus, my famous uncle continues to need our prayers.*

LABOR DAY

A Labor Day Hymn

We thank You Lord
for the meaning you place on our labor.
More than an income,
our jobs offer blessings to savor.
Paychecks and perks.
Chances to trust You at work.
Bosses with whom we have favor.

We thank You Lord
for all doctors and nurses and teachers.
Real estate agents, computer programmers
and preachers.
Librarians, mail carriers, firemen.
Those who write daily sports features.

We thank You Lord that our work is a holy vocation.
In what we do we are offering You an oblation.
Priests all are we. So claims our theology.
Work gives our witness occasion.

We thank You Lord for the privilege
of honest employment.
Having a job is a gift having faced unemployment.
Though at times stressed,
in what I do I'll be blessed
if I see it as deployment.

(tune: Praise to the Lord, the Almighty)

PATRIOT DAY

A Patriot Day Prayer

Seven years? Already? Wow!
The time has flown and yet somehow
we've coined a day to call to mind
an unseen enemy.

Today we think of those who died
in a Pennsylvania countryside
and those perished in New York,
as well as in D.C.

We honor those who lost their lives,
whose friends and families were deprived
of spouses, children, moms and dads...
because of terrorists.

Lord, thank you for these patriots,
for firefighters, heroes, cops.
For average folks who had no clue
that day would be their last.

Please comfort families who still grieve
and grant them faith so they'll believe
their loved ones did not die in vain
but left a legacy.

The Misnomer of Ground Zero

Ground Zero is already eight.
A birthday that recalls
a more innocent time
when terrorists robbed our nation
of its child-like trust
and assumed sense of safety.

Ground Zero is 9/11.
A grave reminder of the day
a pair of twins collapsed
and perished
while Mother Liberty
looked on in horror.

Ground Zero is a misnomer.
It is anything but
nothing, nada, zippo.
It's blood-soaked soil
that hides seeds of hatred
fertilized by memories of anguish.

Ground Zero is nonetheless
hallowed ground near a market
whose stock and trade
continues to be carried out
in the shadow of a skyline
in which two notable towers
are sadly missing.

Ground Zero remains
the face of a nation
whose ability to smile
has forever been altered,
like an eight-year-old missing
her two front teeth.

ELECTION DAY

An Election Day Prayer

On this day, our Father, as we take a stand,
we kneel at the outset to pray for our land.

You've given us freedom to worship and pray,
as well as to choose those who see things Your way.

With thanks for the Rights that our forefathers wrote,
we're grateful, dear God, for the privilege to vote.

The campaigning's over. The words-war is past.
The day for deciding is here at long last.

Assist those officials in each polling place.
Imbue them with patience and smiles on each face.

Keep systems from failing and shysters from fraud.
In all of the details, be present, O God.

Prompt those apathetic to break from routines
that keep them from levers and voting machines.

When we cast our ballots, please help us think straight,
quite mindful of what we should value and hate.

We're asking that those who revere You will win.
Our nation needs leaders who won't wink at sin.

Because there's so much that is really at stake,
accomplish Your plans through the choices we make.

As totals are tallied and losers concede,
be near them and comfort their hearts as they bleed.

Remind those victorious they answer to You
in laws that they pass and in all that they do.

And as this Election Day draws to a close,
help us to make peace with the outcomes we chose.
Amen.

An Election Day Intercession

Decision Day will soon be here
when we must take a stand.
Remind us, Lord, that we aren't simply
voting for a man.

Our choice will welcome policies,
initiatives and planks
that form a platform of ideals.
But, Lord, may I be frank?
I am discouraged by the trend

to leave our faith at home.
We need You standing by our side.
We dare not vote alone.

Please grant us wisdom as we mark
our ballots next Tuesday.
And may the outcome be the means
to serve Your will I pray.

Election Day in Who-ville

Election Day in Who-ville
finds the Grinch much like a goat.
He butts and taunts his neighbors
who are headed off to vote.

"Don't waste your time! It's foolish!"
Mr. Grinch is heard to chide.
"Casting ballots is baloney.
All you get is civic pride.

"Do you really think that what you mark
and drop inside a drum
will help elect your candidate
when all is said and done?

"And do you think the issues
that you're so worked up about
will be decided by YOUR vote?
I doubt you have that clout!"

Yet all the while the Grinch well knows
how much elections mean.
It is a fact he must admit
(just like the fact he's green).

Deep in his heart he knows the truth
about democracy.
Until we start to vote ourselves,
we lack integrity.

He knows we fight to give the world
our form of government.
But if we fail to practice it,
we prove we're impudent.

Paying Our Dues

Election Day gives us a choice
to give our values wings and voice.
It's spending time to pay respect
to what makes freedom ring.

When we neglect our treasured right,
we fail to leverage godly might.
When we forget or just don't vote,
we leech off liberty.

Yes, voting is like paying dues.
We mark our ballots and we choose.
And in the process we invest
in funding freedom's cost.

VETERANS' DAY

Funding Our Troops on Our Knees

While Congress funds our troops at war,
there's still a debt to pay.
It's what is due that has a cost.
We pay it when we pray.

Our prayer support means so much more
than what reporters say.
Our boys and girls in uniform
find comfort when we pray.

Because these freedom fighters
are entangled in the fray,
we can't ignore a bill past-due.
God hears us when we pray.

Each One a Hero

On this day each November
I urge you to recall
the ones who served our Uncle Sam
while proudly standing tall.

Fatigued and dressed for battle,
they marched into harm's way
so freedom's flag might always fly.
They knew the price they'd pay.

Some died and some were wounded.
Some came home without limbs.
Some found God in a foxhole prayer
while some lost faith in Him.

Each one is someone's hero.
Each one deserves our thanks.
They risked their lives with brave resolve
on ships, in jets or tanks.

Before this day is over,
be sure that you reflect
on what we owe this dying breed
whose service we neglect.

Remember to Say Thanks

"Now, don't forget," my mother urged.
"Remember to say thanks."
She taught me those four magic words
when I was prone to pranks.

I've thought about my mom's advice
quite often since I've grown.
Her simple words were quite profound.
Their truth is clearly shown.

When I recall what soldiers did
to keep our nation free,
my sense of gratitude's renewed
for those who fought for me.

When I reflect on those in town
who wear a uniform,
my mind replays the risks they take
to keep me safe and warm.

When we remember, heroes live.
When we forget, they die.
Remembering births gratitude,
although it makes us cry.

So let's remember to give thanks.
You won't if you forget.
Thank God for veterans you have known
and those you've never met.

The Old Marine

The old Marine is weak and tired.
He's earned the right to rest.
His furrowed brow can now relax.
He's faced his final test.

His wrinkled hands appear at peace.
They clutch a wooden cross.
This old Marine knows all too well
that winning follows loss.

I watch him take his final breath.
Then peacefully he's gone.
A long-awaited victory
at last has finally come.

And like that Iwo Jima mount
where brave men raised a flag,
a banner flies in Heaven now
as all the angels brag

about redemption's victory
as blood ran down a hill
when one brave man gave up his life
in keeping with God's will.

With eyes of faith I see it all.
The old Marine's at peace.
As "Semper Fi" rings in his ears,
he finds his soul's release.

** I wrote this poem about my dad as he slipped into a coma
from which he would not awaken. My dad was a proud Marine
who had the distinct privilege of being an honor guard aboard
the U.S.S. Missouri at the ceremony that ended World War 2.
He would have been pleased to know his memorial service
coincided with the 233rd birthday of the Marine Corps. Semper
Fi is the Marines' motto which means "always faithful." I
believe the first words my father heard as he entered into the
presence of his Lord were "well done, good and faithful
servant…" That is Heaven's paraphrase of "Semper Fi."*

THANKSGIVING

Recipe for a Grateful Heart
Food for thought on Thanksgiving Day.

My ability in writing books is not matched by my
ability to read a cookbook. My wife and three daughters
will attest to that. Except for popping corn and blending
chocolate milkshakes, most of my efforts in the kitchen
taste like mistakes.

But don't be too quick to label me as a liability when it
comes to preparing for the family Thanksgiving feast. In
the five decades of life in which I've had the opportunity
to digest my share of what the Lord has served up in my
life, I've discovered a fail-proof recipe for a grateful heart.

First, crush a bunch of sour grapes for all the times
you've felt someone else got credit for something you
deserved. Drizzle in a drop of spilled milk for every

remembrance you have of something you wish you could undo (no need to cry over it). Even though you may be tempted to, refrain from adding the "whine" you keep in the cellar for those pity parties you occasionally throw for yourself.

To this rather unattractive concoction, sift in some flavorful thoughts that come to mind of times when God was kind and bailed you out. You know the times I mean: when you were in real hot water and had real doubts if you could stand up to the heat.

Then, while this mixture is sitting at room temperature, take some "thyme" alone and thoroughly measure out your blessings. Make sure you add in the plain vanilla ones (like health, shelter, employment, family, enough to eat and a good night's sleep).

Don't forget to spoon up some sweet remembrances of happy days gone by. With your honey at your side, go to a quiet part of the house and pour out what's on your mind. If necessary, ask for forgiveness.

While bringing the ingredients to a boil, combine a cup full of contentment, all the while skimming off any envy or greed which surfaces. Blend well.

Let the aforementioned batter rise until it occupies a place of prominence in your thinking. Preheat your heart to the point where it takes on a pliable consistency. While your will is warming to the idea of thanking God (instead of blaming him) for where you are at this time in your life, sprinkle the mixture in question with a dash of determination to do whatever it takes to honor God with your attitude.

Then bake the combined ingredients until they are well done. While it is still warm, serve yourself the "peace" you've anticipated, all the while chewing on God's goodness while swallowing your pride.

Well, there you have it. Even though you haven't seen

this recipe demonstrated on the Food Network, it's a keeper. A grateful heart is guaranteed.

You don't need to be a Galloping Gourmet in order to serve up an aroma that will be pleasing to the Lord. All that is required is that you dismount from your high horse of self-centeredness and sit in the presence of the One from whom all blessings flow. As Israel's greatest king is credited with having said, "Taste and see that the Lord is good." (Psalm 34:8)

Lord, We Are Grateful

Lord, we are grateful for all you've given;
shelter and clothing, good food and health.
All these are gifts we rarely do treasure.
We are most wealthy, thanks to Yourself.

Lord, we are grateful for those who love us;
those we call family, those who are friends.
Loved, we can face the pressures life sends us.
Through those we cherish, Your love descends.

Lord, we are grateful for Your creation;
trees in fall splendor, dark stormy skies.
Nature reminds us of Your strong power.
Majestic beauty dazzles ours eyes.

Lord, we are grateful for Your rich mercy,
fresh as the morning, new every day.
Sin is forgiven. Guilt has been buried.
Gone is the debt we never could pay.

Lord, we are grateful that we can worship,
often and freely here in this place.
Harvest our praises. Hear our thanksgiving
as we reflect on Your awesome grace.

(tune: Morning Has Broken)

With Thanks for Blessings

O God, we pause acknowledging Your goodness.
Our lives are rich in spite of what we own.
Our wealth is found in being called Your children.
In taking stock of love that's found at home.
We're grateful for retirement and pensions.
For daily jobs at which our skills are known.

Accept our thanks for blessings You've provided.
For all the ways You cancel out our needs.
For nourishment that satisfies our hunger.
For living in a nation that is free.
And for Your Son, who gave His life to save us
that we might live with You eternally.

(tune: Finlandia)

Receive Our Thanks

Receive our thanks for what is on our table.
Our thirsts are quenched, our appetites are filled
(both physical and spiritual provision).
And all because Your grace, O God, has willed
that we be fed in spirit, mind and body
and that our restless search for You be stilled.

America is our Creator's canvas
on which He's painted quite a wonderland.
With awe we contemplate creation's beauty.
Five lakes called great and one deep canyon grand.
The Rocky Mountains and the windswept prairies,
Alaska's tundra and Mojave's sand.

O God, we bow in penitential sorrow,
confessing our resistance to Your way.
We've left undone the good that was our duty
while we have done our best to disobey.
We've let our culture dictate norms and values
and dodged Truth's debt that one day we must pay.

Forgive us, Lord. We have no hope without You.
Absolve the guilt our nation has incurred.
Remove the stain of corporate transgressions.
Remind us, God, that prayers (through faith) are heard.
Restore the values that once marked our country.
Revive our souls and may our hearts be stirred.

(Tune: Finlandia)

Late Is My Gratefulness

Late is my gratefulness, O God my Father.
I'm tardy thanking You for what You've done.
Daily You've given me countless reminders
of Your great faithfulness, Most Faithful One.

Refrain:
Late is my gratefulness. Late is my gratefulness.
Forgive my tardiness honoring You.
I've been remiss in recalling Your goodness.
Your steadfast mercies, Lord, are ever new.

Late is my gratefulness, O God my Father.
I have been careless extolling Your care.
Daytime or nighttime, Your grace like a blanket
covers me gently. Your love's everywhere. (*Refrain*)

Late is my gratefulness, O God my Father.
I've no excuse for my ingratitude.
I beg forgiveness for failing to praise You.
Great is Your faithfulness in all You do. (*Refrain*)

(Tune: Great Is Thy Faithfulness)

With Thanks for Thanksgiving
What makes this holiday my favorite.

A feathered beast. A family feast.
Some football and some pie.
Thanksgiving is MY holiday
and here are reasons why.

It is the day I'm free to pray
at church OR City Hall.
The need to show God gratitude
seems natural to all.

My wife's great food. My brother's brood.
And time to just relax.
This priceless day is one fine gift
my Uncle Sam can't tax.

A lazy walk around the block.
A nap when I feel tired.
A game of Scrabble (Skipbo too)
and popcorn by the fire.

Simplicity (it seems to me)
describes this holiday.
No gifts to buy (or to return).
No customs to obey.

This day of thanks with beans and franks
would still be just as great.
What makes Thanksgiving what I love
is more than what I ate.

Giving Thanks in Hard Times

This is a day for giving thanks,
for taking stock and such.
But frankly, Lord, the news is bleak.
We don't have quite as much.

Though winds of change are heard to howl
and leave us feeling cold,
remind us, Father, of the facts
Your ancient prophets told.

Economies will rise and fall,
securities give way.
But You are faithful like the dawn
with mercies new each day.

Just like the pilgrims long ago,
we bow our heads in prayer.
We're thankful, Lord, that in hard times
we have enough to share.

HOLY DAYS

The Day Before Christmas

It's the day before Christmas
and your shopping's not done.
You've maxed out the VISA and Capital One.
Your kids are expecting a flat-screen TV,
a Tivo, an X-box and even a Wii.

They have no idea how bad things have got
and how much your stomach's all tied up in knots.
The market is iffy. Your job's insecure,
and plans for next summer have lost their allure.

The Spirit of Christmas seems way beyond reach.
It's like you've been drained by a joy-sucking leech.
In twenty-four hours the big day arrives;
and like old man Scrooge,
your heart's shriveled in size.

But lest you give up and turn into the Grinch,
consider this game plan to ease Humbug's pinch.

Just take time to chill out. Warm up by the fire.
Then prayerfully ponder your heartfelt desire
to count all your blessings that money can't buy.
Like children who hug you and puppies that try.
The vows at your wedding. Your mate's faithfulness.
Their mute understanding and tender caress.
A bank full of memories that no one can rob.
Your grandfather's watch with his antique gold fob.
The wealth of true friendship.

A chum's knowing glance.
And when you have screwed up,
that prized second chance.
A healthy awareness of all you can do.
Those talents God gave you that help define you.

That fireside reflection should brighten your mood.
By adding up blessings, you start feeling good.
In spite of these hard times, recession and debt,
you're really quite wealthy. You tend to forget
that *Joy to the World* is much more than a song.
It's what you can give
even when you've been wronged.
When you feel content without lusting for more,
you give from your heart, not some shelf at a store.
The best gifts you wrap aren't expensive you see.
They're priceless and costly and yet they are free.

That brings us to Christmas. That miracle birth.
A young virgin mother who doubted her worth.
The manger. The angels. The shepherds who came.
A baby long-promised to free us from shame.
A human-wrapped present no one could afford
was offered without charge. That babe was the Lord.
That's it in a nutshell. He's God's gift of love.

The Present (or Presence) we all have dreamed of.
Amazingly awesome. Too good to be true.
Attempts to earn Heaven are over. They're through.

So don't sweat tomorrow. Just let Christmas come.
In light of its message, be grateful. Have fun.
Expect imperfection. Accept what you get.
Be thankful and patient. Let go of regrets.
Give grace when offended. Extend tenderness.
And when the day's over your soul will feel blest.

A Christmas Call to Worship

Angels from heaven hovered in silence
over a hill where men guarded sheep.
Then without warning they began singing,
"Glorify God who grants us His peace."

Silent night broken, shepherds quite frightened
rushed to the stable where Jesus slept.
Kneeling in worship, awestruck with wonder,
Lamb-of-God finders joyfully wept.

Magi from Persia journeyed by camel
in search of crowning one born a king.
And upon reaching Israel's Messiah,
they offered homage, spice, and gold rings.

Angels and shepherds and magi model
pure adoration, simple yet true.
In their example we're called to worship.
This ancient story is ever new.

Christmas continues after December,
as does the worship Jesus is due.
Sensing His presence, we can't keep silent.
Our God is with us all the year through.

My Christmas List

This Christmas finds me pondering
the things I'm hoping for.
Like boosting the economy
and finishing the war.

I hope that our new President
will take his cues from God
so he's not swayed by what's "PC,"
though criticized as odd.

I want to help the homeless find
a decent place to sleep,
to feed them and to help them land
a job they'll want to keep.

I wish for all who've lost someone
to cancer's deadly curse,
good memories of more pleasant days
before they became worse.

I long for shorter time between
those visits with my mom.
I pray she'll live for many years
before I hear "She's gone."

I hope my kids will find a mate
who values what they're worth.
I want all careless litterbugs
to care for Mother Earth.

I pray that people 'round the world
will search within their hearts
to find the Father's fingerprints
in nature and the arts.

I long to see inventive minds
reduce the spread of AIDS.
I hope that new technologies
reverse mistakes we've made.

I have a dream that what God willed
in sending Christ to us
will be fulfilled as evidenced
by peace, goodwill and trust.

And on a much more lighter note,
I want my team to win.
I want to lose a few more pounds.
A few more? How 'bout ten?

I wish for strength to push away
that second slice of pie,
and courage to ask "What's your name?"
when tempted to be shy.

As you can see, what's on my list
are things I cannot buy.
But still, I think they're possible
if, with God's help, we try.

Homeless at Christmastime

In need of shelter, food and clothes,
a homeless couple nearly froze
while wandering from door to door.
They wondered if God cared.

Their plight was caused by government
that taxed them poor and stole their rent.
Each night they faced the humbling task
of looking for a bed.

Do you recognize them?
Do you know their names?

A baby fills the woman's womb.
She knows delivery will be soon.
But what she doesn't know is where
her labor will conclude.

Both she and her young husband find
the world is prejudiced and blind
to those in need, whose lot in life
is not what meets the eye.

And yet not everyone's the same.
Unwilling to attribute shame
to these whose need can't be denied,
an unnamed man responds.

When posed the Starbucks' question "Room?"
he sees two faces framed by gloom
and makes the effort to make space
before the two are three.

A Christmas Wish

There are those things we dread in life
we can't always control,
like family wounds and old regrets
that fester in the soul.

They kill the joy and steal the peace
that Christ was born to give.
And bandaged hearts long bruised by hurts
hold love much like a sieve.

If we could only find a way
to make a brand new start,
my Christmas would be most complete.
I'll gladly do my part.

A Call for Compassion

When darkness falls, where will he sleep?
The hill that leads to help is steep.
And since he's weak and lacks the strength,
he makes the street his bed.

Her face is stained by sweat and tears.
Her eyes reflect unstated fears
that stalk her hopes and dreams each night
and greet her with the dawn.

Where will they go? Can help be found?
Or will they curl up on the ground
in some deserted alley way
or on a vacant bench?

The need is great. The cost quite small
when what it takes is shared by all.
And when we give to serve the least,
we benefit the most.

So when appeals come in the mail
or bells are rung beside a pail,
resist the urge to blow them off.
Remember, times are hard.

My Dad Went Home for Christmas

My dad went home for Christmas.
The Father welcomed him.
The lights of Heaven twinkled bright
as he was ushered in.

The little drummer boy marked time.
My dad knew he belonged.
He met the shepherds, saw the Lamb
and heard the angels' song.

He bowed and worshiped Jesus Christ,
the greatest gift of all,
the object of my dear dad's faith
from when he was quite small.

That's why when he got really sick,
he had the means to hope.
Aware the Father's plans are good,
he found that he could cope.

He coped with all that cancer dealt,
relinquished to God's will.
He said he was all set to go
before his voice was stilled.

But, boy, these silent nights are hard.
This Christmas will be rough
in spite of knowing Dad's now whole.
Alive, all smiles and buffed.

A Christmastime Prayer for Our Troops

O, God, be near our troops today.
Homesick, they are well aware
that their place at the family table
will lack their presence this year.
They also know that their presents
'neath the Christmas tree
will have to wait for a later date.

In the meantime, Father,
give them reason
in this season of Immanuel
to sense God-with-us with them.

Remind them that peace on earth
is worth their frontline courage
as well as the sacrifices
they may be called to make.

Although the carols they try to sing
may catch in their throats,
allow them to swallow
their current circumstances
without bitterness or regret.

As these men and women sing *Joy to the World*,
help them to know happiness in their hearts.
May the letters, e-mails and phone calls they receive
be tidings of comfort and joy.

And although the explosive nights in a war zone
are anything but silent,
give these who serve global justice
freedom from terror-triggered nightmares
and the ability to dream of goodwill to men.
In the name of the Prince of Peace we pray. Amen

This is the Season

This is the season for hope and love.
Christ is the reason sent from above.
There in the manger, God showed His face,
cooing His mercy, whispering grace.

Refrain:
This is the season. Christmas is here.
Come let us worship, from far and near.
No longer distant, God is with us.
The waiting's over. Christmas at last.

This is the season for joy and peace.
Twinkle lights signal conflicts to cease.
Offer forgiveness. Warmly embrace.
Share a broad smile. Give happiness.

(Refrain)

This is the season for gifts and such.
Symbols of friendship that cost so much.
God's gift of Jesus cost Him far more.
This priceless package, let us adore.

(Refrain)

(tune: Blessed Assurance)

This Jesus

Within the Book we see the Man
to whom all history pointed.
His words of truth and healing touch
proved He was God's anointed.

He is the Savior of mankind
who by the curse to grace are blind.
This Jesus is God's answer.

In Him we hear the Father's heart
that pulses with compassion.
It is a heartbeat for the poor
who aren't enslaved by fashion.

He stands with those unjustly framed
and those denied both wealth and fame.
This Jesus is God-with-us.

In Him we find our only hope
when all we treasure crumbles.
He promises the means to stand
when pridefully we stumble.

He offers joy, not happiness.
Significance, not mere success.
This Jesus is God's wisdom.

(tune: Sing Praise to God Who Reigns Above)

Babe in a Manger

Babe in a manger, Bethlehem stranger.
See our Creator cradled in straw.
In this small child so undefiled,
grace flows to sinners helplessly flawed.

There where You're lying, I hear You crying.
Your little forehead wrinkled in pain.
Son of the Father, why are You bothered?
Are You aware You'll die for our shame?

Shepherds and magi, what in the night sky
caused you to leave your sheep and your land?
Was it your hunger for cosmic wonder?
Or was it hope of touching God's hand?

Joseph and Mary, wasn't it scary
fleeing from Herod's ego-born rage?
Although discouraged, you modeled courage
braving the desert with faith uncaged.

Is it amazing that we are praising
One who was born to set our souls free?
No, it is Christmas and God is with us.
Worship's our calling eternally.

(tune: Morning Has Broken)

Christianity #101

Unlike Muslims, Jews or Sikhs,
what makes Christ-followers unique
is that they think there's just one way
that they can get to God

And though that may seem strange to some,
just think of dialing 9-1-1.
When you're in need, there's just one call
that's sure to get you help.

For God so loved the world He came
to be a human with a name,
to take the rap for what we've done
and take away our guilt.

While some think you can earn your way,
that's not what you'll hear Christians say.
They are convinced that what God's done
is all that is required.

So when it all is said and done,
what matters most is that God's Son
was born and died and came to life
that we might know we're loved.

It's a Wonderful Life

It's a wonderful life. Everyday is a gift.
There's wonder in all that I see.
From a sunrise at dawn to a moonscape at dusk,
I'm wealthy as wealthy can be.

Refrain:
A wonderful life I've been giv'n.
It's almost like being in Heav'n.
Everyday God is near so I've nothing to fear.
A wonderful life He gives me.

It's a wonderful life, be it sunshine or rain,
for beauty is found everywhere.
In a spouse's embrace or a grandchild's face,
I treasure these treasures most rare. (*Refrain*)

It's a wonderful life knowing that I am loved,
that Jesus has died for my sin.
All the guilt and regrets that once shadowed my past
need never resurface again. (*Refrain*)

(tune: Since Jesus Came Into My Heart)

* I wrote the above lyrics to be sung at our church the Sunday that Karolyn Grimes shared her faith-journey in the service. Karolyn was the child actress who played Zuzu Bailey in the classic Christmas movie "It's a Wonderful Life."

Embracing Grace

Reaching my arms around the Christmas Child,
I reach the destination of humanity's Magi-like journey
for which I was born (for which He was born).

As I cradle the infant King,
the cadence of my pounding heart increases.
This little One who clasps my thumb with tiny fingers
is no ordinary baby. These same fingers
once flung a billion stars into space.

But that was long ago and far away.
That was before an orbiting earth
became a revolving stage on which two actors fell,
causing their opening night
to become our endless nightmare.
A stand-in was required.
"And the Word became flesh and dwelt among us."

Though His performance of a lifetime
resulted in mixed reviews,
His work on Calvary allowed redemption's play
to reach the final act.

Embracing God's grace,
I hold Emmanuel in my arms
and find the faith to face tomorrow.
After all, in spite of Eden's fall,
God is with me.

A Prayer for Christmas Grace

The day the family gathers
for our yearly Christmas feast
I pray for Heaven's mercies,
lest I turn into a beast.

Sister tells a story
that demeans a certain race,
while cousin Ken consistently
puts fat folks in their place.

Grandpa Gus begins to snore
in a rocking chair that creaks.
My brother, Joe, just doesn't know
how much his BO reeks.

Aunt Andrea arrives too late
to help out in the kitchen;
And based on Uncle Bradley's breath,
you know what he's been nippin'.

The nephews are a nuisance.
The nieces can't sit still.
Grandma gripes about the noise
while choking on her pills.

Still, Christmas is for families.
I know that in my head.
But when it comes to joining them,
I'd rather stay in bed.

An Epiphany Prayer

We don't know their number
We don't know their names.
But we do know what they gave.
And to Whom.
Although anonymous,
those ancient star-gazers
gave the infant King
the very thing
He desires from us.
And so, dear God,
give us the desire to offer Jesus
the worship of our hearts
that is expressed through
the currency of our worth,
the fragrance of sweet dispositions
and the spice of graciousness
that covers the decay of others imperfections.

On this Epiphany Day
I pray that I would be more like the magi, Lord.
Determined to go the distance,
no matter how difficult
or how long the journey might be each day,
to spend time in Your presence
and offer You the essence of my love.
Orient my perspective, please,
that I might seize every opportunity
to be conformed to the image of Christ.
In His name, I pray. Amen

Modern-Day Magi

Daughters, sons of Abraham,
scan the sky because I AM
has promised to be found by those
who seek with hearts to find.

Muslim, Jew and Christian too,
share a common past, it's true.
But all three kings of worship-dom
do not share common ground.

Only those made wise by grace
drop to their knees, fall on their face
and offer gifts beyond their means
because no less will do.

But the number of those grows.
Seekers still seek.
Askers keep asking why.
And magi, discontent
with unreasoned answers,

continue to dismount
from their high horses of pride
and inbred prejudice
in order to make their way
to a manger of mystery
where in the cradle of divine disclosure
the one true God is seen
(camouflaged in humanity).

And we are the modern-day magi.
I and you,
who, as those before us,
fall on our faces
and offer our worship
to the One who in time
every knee will acknowledge...
wise men and foolish ones,
dark skinned and lighter hues,
of Israel and Islam and Buddha too.
For in the crude stable
lies the only means able
to lift us (forgiven) to God.
To the seed of Father Abraham,
to the Son of King David,
to the Savior of all humankind,
we magi bow in praise.

GOOD FRIDAY AND EASTER

Passover Table Grace

It was an upper room like this one
where Jesus gathered with his friends
for a Passover like no other...

with a spin.
Christ died for us. Christ was buried.
Christ now lives again.

He's still providing for our hunger.
He is God's answer to our sin.

And so this Passover and Easter,
we contemplate how rich we are.
Fiddlers and Tevyes together
join our choir.
Christ died for us. Christ was buried.
Christ now lives again.
With His blood brushed upon our hearts' doors,
we have no fear of death within.

He gave the bread and cup new meaning.
In both the matzo and the wine,
we see a picture of Christ's passion
one more time.
Christ died for us. Christ was buried.
Christ now lives again.
Passover morphs into Good Friday
and then we sing an Easter hymn.

(tune: Sunrise, Sunset from "Fiddler on the Roof")

A Good Friday Lesson at St. Arbucks

How a Tacoma barista showed Christ's love.

Baristas are a giving breed.
They look for ways to meet a need.
Most slake our thirst for coffee drinks.
But Sandie did much more.

She gave the gift of life to one
whose transplant hopes were slim to none.
And when reporters asked her why,
she smiled and said, "Why not?"

St. Arbucks proudly claims Sandie
who gave her kidney selflessly
to save this "short drip double-cup"
because she was her type.

Baristas come. Baristas go.
And yet it's clear, I hope you know,
that there's a Christ-like show of love
in what this woman did.

She took a risk and shed her blood
(more precious than a cup of mud).
She bore her cross in surgery
and put another first.

* On March 11, 2008 Barista Sandie Andersen was wheeled
into surgery to give one of her kidneys to Annamarie Ausnes,
one of her regular customers at a Tacoma, Washington
Starbucks, who needed a new kidney to survive.

The Way of Suffering

The Via Dolorosa
is a familiar road winding through
the old city of Jerusalem.
It has known the footsteps of a carpenter,
the hoof-prints of a donkey
and the imprint of a cross

that bounced while dragged
across its sun-baked cobblestones.
Palms, once green and waved
with joy and jubilation,
now line the road all brown and brittle,
crushed by apathetic feet.
Appropriate, perhaps,
given what would soon take place
(where this avenue of agony dead-ends
outside the city gates) on a hill
on a cross.

I Thirst

Is it possible that He who claimed to be living water...
Is it possible that He who said, *"Come unto Me and drink..."*
Is it possible that He who told the Samaritan woman
that He had water she knew nothing about...
Is it possible that this Man could mouth the words,
"I thirst"?

And because He did, the incarnation message of Christmas
is voiced in this human cry of Good Friday.
Jesus, the divine Creator of life,
is now subject to the creation and the creature's basic needs.
Yes, Jesus, the Son of God, actually needed water.
For six hours He hung from a calloused cross on a hot, barren hill
beneath a darkened middle-eastern sky.

He was bleeding profusely and losing vital body fluids.
What is more, without sleep the night before,
without food or drink, He had been tortured, teased
and tried before a tribunal

before the crucifixion had even begun.
His lips were parched, His tongue swollen
as He managed to blurt out His human thirst...
A thirst that spoke of His total identification with all our needs,
drives, hopes and sufferings.

Jesus' physical thirst only symbolized the deeper thirsts
that every human being who has ever lived has felt:
the thirst for companionship,
the thirst for acceptance,
the thirst for immortality,
the thirst for end to suffering,
and most importantly,
the thirst for relationship with God.

Augustine said it centuries ago:
"Thou hast made me for thyself, O God
And I am restless till I rest in Thee."
But the Psalmist said it long before Augustine:
"As the deer pants for flowing streams,
so thirsts my soul for Thee, O God."

A restlessness, a panting,
a thirst to end all thirsts,
a thirst no water, no wine,
no gall could ever quench.

And for once Jesus knew that desire of all ages Himself.

As the bearer of all sin
of all people of all time,
Jesus knew the separation and desperation
that all creation has known apart from God.
And He cried, "I thirst."

The Baby of Bethlehem.
The Christ of the Cross
knows the creature's cage.
He's acquainted with our pain,
our pressures, our panic,
our plight apart from the Father.

And because He's been there,
He knows how to quench our thirst.

** This was the first poem I ever had published in a Christian
periodical. It first appeared in print in "The Pentecostal
Evangel" March 27, 1988.*

The Red Sea (Revisited)

It was called "the exodus."
An exit ramp leading from a dead-end street
to a freeway of sorts.
A nation of indentured brick makers,
bricklayers and pyramid polishers
(finally freed by a pharaoh guilty of infanticide)
packed up and headed east.
The Red Sea parted and the dust flew
as six million sandaled feet forward-marched.

A dry ocean floor became an interstate
to a promised land for which God's chosen
had waited for four hundred years.

"The exodus" is a timeless story of redemption.
But the events surrounding the Red Sea crossing
of an enclave of Hebrew slaves
does not comprise the whole story.

Yes, the Red Sea was a highway to Sinai.
It was a dry way to freedom.
But it isn't the only Red Sea
in which we see God at work.

Where is Paul Harvey when you need him?
The rest of the story is dying to be told.
It's a novel ending begging to be read.
And today is the day to do just that.

As Christ clung to life and stared at death
(hanging from two crossbeams
and between two thieves),
His blood trickled like tributaries
from ruptured arteries and veins.
The leaking red elixir of life
became a river of death
flowing downward from His writhing body
to the foot of His cross.
Because the crimson-stained ground
was soon saturated by the constant stream
(from a spotless sacrificial Lamb
Moses never imagined),
the blood pooled into a sea of red.

In that crimson tide of blood
we find a second Red Sea.
It stands between us
and God's promised redemption,
forgiveness, freedom, abundant life
and inner peace.

Until we cross this sea of red,
we are slaves to sin and selfish motives.
Until we get across it,

we are in bondage to self-destructive
behaviors and attitudes.
Yet this bloody barrier
gives us cause for pause.

Just as the people of God
contemplated their options
as they encountered the first sea of red,
so we must determine our course of action.
Will we step forward?
Or will we just stand there?
Will we advance? Or will we retreat?

In all honesty,
there are reasons to resist taking the plunge.
Doubt, pride, disbelief, feelings of unworthiness
and rationalized feelings of contentment
with the old life.

Unlike the original Red Sea crossing,
those who step into the crimson waves
will not find a dry sea bed on which to travel.
No mighty wind and miracle divide this time.
The decision to move forward will mean
total immersion and a process of dyeing.
Those who emerge on the other side of the sea
are red-stained but clothed
in the righteousness of Christ

As such they are certified as citizens
in the land of God's promise.
A land the Bible calls the Kingdom of God.

A Purpose-Driven Death (and Life)

Why Good Friday Depends on Great Sunday.

His was a purpose-driven life.
He had no wealth. He had no wife.
He didn't write a must-read book.
He lacked a photogenic look.
Compared with how we judge success,
He didn't score too high.

And though He didn't know much fame,
this man stayed true to why He came.
He hung with those considered lost
and then He hung upon a cross.
Because mankind is evil-prone,
this kind man chose to die.

Still Jesus' aim was not fulfilled
when Friday came and He was killed.
To prove His love can make us new,
He had a bit more work to do.
His purpose-driven life would fail
if Death had the last word.

But there was much more to be said
by one who spoke, although quite dead.
And He whose words first birthed the world
escaped the grave, its clothes unfurled,
to show that what He'd come to do
was definitely done.

The Gospel According to Mel

A word study of The Passion of the Christ.

helping
healing
teaching grace
fasting
feasting
making space

tempted
tested
seeking God
prayerful
pensive
sweating blood

labeled
libeled
slandered wrong
bullied
broken
punished long

pounded
pummeled
bleeding red
hammered
hated
dying dead

silenced
staggered
you and me
guilty
grateful
finally free

The Passion of the Christ

Why Jesus would be a guest on The Ellen Degeneres Show.

Oh, by the way, I heard that Mel
was on the Ellen Show.
Their passions are not quite the same.
He's hetero you know.

A Gibson girl this host is not.
We all know Ellen's gay.
And Mel's a bloody Jesus chap
who claims the narrow way.

But lest you judge the actor's choice
for being Ellen's guest,
consider what you know of Christ.
Let that be Prudent's test.

This rabbi ate with prostitutes.
He hung with the maligned
while those self-righteous holy types
were hateful and unkind.

Though criticized, the rabbi loved
to mix with those who sinned.
In fact, the Good Book clearly states
he was the sinners' friend.

The bottom line? I think J.C.
would sit at Ellen's side.
The passion of the Christ was love
and that is why He died.

The Fellowship of Feet

Before the traitor had taken off,
Jesus humbled Himself
before twelve pair of familiar feet.
Feet that had run with delight in His direction
when He had first nodded in theirs.
Feet that had walked with Him
for the better part of three years
on 'a long obedience in the same direction.'
Feet that had remained on a narrow path
far removed from a broader (more popular) road.
Feet that had stumbled on stones
thrown by critics who questioned
their determined allegiance to a carpenter-turned-rabbi.
Feet calloused by the number of times
they had squashed their doubts and trudged on in faith.
Feet that (ironically) still longed
to climb the rungs of self-importance
in hopes of landing on a pedestal of glory.
Feet smudged by the mud of daily compromise,
smelling of imperfect devotion.
Feet that would soon flee in fear
when the feet (and hands)
of their Righteous Friend
were nailed to a Roman cross.
Beautiful feet that (with the exception of one pair)
would in time climb the mountains of the earth,
finding their ultimate worth,
declaring the incredible good news that our God reigns!
It was these feet the Savior cradled with compassion
as He rinsed and toweled them dry.
It was this amazing act of undeserved humility
and unforgettable grace
that Jesus commanded His friends to emulate.
And to that end we lace up our shoes
and follow in His footsteps
in the shadow of His cross.

A Grave Mistake

Unearthing Jesus is a seasonal disorder.

The bones of Jesus in a box?
His wife and son as well?
If true, our faith is but a farce
and we're all bound for hell.

For Heaven's sake! This grave ordeal
is only "holy" hype.
It's just the game Christ's critics play.
You know their rules and type.

The headlines claim He didn't rise.
It happens every year.
The media discredits faith
as Holy Week draws near.

The skeptics can't accept the fact
that Easter might be true.
They dig up ways to make their case.
It's really nothing new.

Unearthing Jesus is the goal
of those who won't believe.
But, boy, it makes me sick inside.
It makes me want to heave.

I wonder what the Savior thinks
at being called a fake.
I'm sure it really breaks His heart.
Eternal life's at stake.

Easter in Disguise

The Son's victory is revealed in Mother Nature.

Disaster loomed. The end seemed sure.
The Lord of life was dead.
Good Friday was a bad nightmare.
The robins chirped their dread.

But like the boy who plugged the dike
to keep a flood at bay,
the Son of God stood up to Death
on resurrection day.

An empty grave means we don't mourn
as those who have no hope.
What Jesus did so long ago
gives us the means to cope.

The nature of this mystery
breaks forth from 'neath the ground.
Creation's rhythm witnesses
to truth Christ's followers found.

The tulips soon will lift their heads
to trumpet Easter's song.
The bulbs we buried in the earth
still live though they seem gone.

In Mother Nature, winter's grief
gives way to joyful spring.
It's Easter's message in disguise.
No wonder millions sing...

"Christ the Lord is risen today!
Alleluia!"

The Mist of Mourning

In the mist that comes with mourning,
in the midst of haunting grief,
the presence of the risen Christ
can offer us relief.

He knows the pain of sorrow.
He feels the ache of loss,
for Jesus tasted death firsthand
upon a lonely cross.

Having tasted death just for our sake,
He swallowed Eden's curse.
And come the dawn of the third day,
He put death in reverse.

He lives to heal our broken hearts.
He lives to offer hope.
He lives to hold us when we're weak
and think we cannot cope.

He lives to plead on our behalf
before the Father's throne.
He lives to chase away our fear
when we feel all alone.

The Sting (Revisited)
Praying Paul Newman made his peace with God.

Old man Newman lost his fight
in the quiet of the night.
A Woodward glance. A star-ward gaze.
A final act on life's small stage.

The sting of death. Grave's victory.
Those blue eyes closed. But did they see
the exodus that God provides
for those who trust Him when they die?

If Jesus became Newman's own,
he learned the truth too few have known.
That guilt is washed by sinless blood,
the guilt of preachers, popes or Hud.

That when Christ did His Easter thing,
He tricked the Devil. That's the sting!
An empty grave means death's reversed
and so is Eden's ancient curse.

*"Where, O death, is your victory? Where, O death, is your
sting?" The sting of death is sin, and the power of sin is the
law. But thanks be to God! He gives us the victory through our
Lord Jesus Christ."*
1 Corinthians 15:55-57

God's Curve

When Christ cried, "It's finished!"
The umpire called, "Strike three!"
Third out. Last up. Game over.
His life was history.
His fans were brokenhearted.
His enemies convinced
that this One with home-run power
would no longer clear the fences.
His bat had been silenced.
His impressive power a distant memory,
His lifeless body abandoned

in a marble-cold dugout.
But the victory dance was short-lived,
when God threw earth a curve.
The One struck out and buried
was back with bat in hand.
God's game plan *had* been followed
for a "world serious" in sin.
For only through His striking out
could Christ's team ever win.

The Ultimate Survivor

Yes, the ultimate Survivor
heard His Father say "You're fired!"
as He buckled 'neath the weight of Calvary's gall.
Though our Jesus was exalted,
He became an Average Joe
in the greatest Trading Spaces of them all.

In His death fear was a factor,
yet He willingly gave in
to the torture all who stood around could see.
When the tribe at last had spoken
and His torch had lost its flame,
this Apprentice offered us immunity.

He was voted off the island
and denied His rightful place,
still He found a way somehow to reappear.
He was fully vindicated
as He put death in its place.
Yes, the ultimate Survivor still is here.

Christ is risen!
He is risen, indeed!

Post-Easter Ponderings

Revisiting a controversial holiday.

Christ is risen!

But isn't evil alive and well as well?
How else can we explain the living Hell
that singes our hope
of sweet dreams for our kids?

A world of Somali pirates,
Sunday school predators,
immigration center snipers
and Wall Street extortionists.

A world of evil, hate and greed
where seeds of corruption
and self-seeking pleasure
are fertilized and germinated
in the soil of an unrestrained society.

Christ is risen!

But is He risen in deeds?
Only to the degree we (His Body)
don work clothes
and work out our salvation
will His resurrection
be made aware
to those who don't really care
about the holiday just past.

Only as we respond
to the felt needs of the lonely,
the marginalized,

and the needy
will our skeptical world
bury its doubts
and give the Church
a second chance

Christ is risen!

But will we rise to the occasion
to raise His standard of righteousness
in our *circle* of relationships,
in the public *square*
and in the *oval* office?

Will we dare to stand up
among those who have considered us
down for the count?

Will we get up
and surprise the crowd
with a life-giving response
to those who sought to do us in?

Will we show up
in places where the power of God
has been written off
as irrelevant and ineffectual?

Will we turn up
the thermostat of love
in a culture that has defined Christ-followers
as cold, heartless and legalistic?

Christ is risen!

HOLY DAYS

But do we treat Him more like
a rosin bag on a pitcher's mound
than the Lord of life?

He can't simply be a quick grab
enabling us to get a firm grip
on our own game
as we proceed to
pitch a new proposal at work,
throw our weight around at church
or wind up in some bases-loaded dilemma.

He insists on being the manager of our lives
who signals from the dugout that
(because of Easter)
it's a whole new ballgame.
A dugout no longer occupied by a dead body
but by living proof that Resurrection Sunday
can't be celebrated just once a year.

Easter is a holiday that impacts
every day of every week of every year.
And to anyone who has ears to hear,
it is a day that has risen to new heights.

Christ is risen!
He is risen, indeed!

BIBLE DAYS

Genesis

The book of beginnings. The first Moses penned
recounting creation, a garden and sin.

A flood and a rainbow. A tower of pride.
A nomad named Abram and Sarah his bride.

A miracle baby. A near sacrifice.
Deception and cunning. Corruption and vice.

The birth of two nations... the Arabs and Jews,
whose ongoing conflict is still in the news.

The twelve boys of Jacob including son, Joe,
who wound up in Egypt. God's will, don't you know?

For when famine threatened, Joe's brothers and dad
found access to Pharaoh through what Joseph had.

The Jacob-sons prospered awaiting God's plan.
They dreamed of God's promise to give them The Land.

Jake's clan was a family of sinners and saints.
They serve as a mirror. Who we are. Who we ain't.

In them we've a picture of our blemished face.
Yes, Genesis offers a glimpse of God's grace.

* Read Genesis 50:15-21
** *I wrote this especially for the Community Bible Study class that meets at our church on Mercer Island.*

In the Beginning

At first there was nothing.
That's all.
Zippo.
Nada.
No brothers or sisters.
No mothers or fodders.

No people. No planets.
No moon and no sun.
Suffice it to say,
'cept for God,
there was none.

But God had a brainstorm.
Eureka! A thought.
I want more to life
than I've currently got.

So He lit up the sky
with a sphere He called moon.
He then made a sun
that shone brightly at noon.

A fitting beginning,
I guess you could say.

The moon reigned at nighttime;
the sun ruled the day.

The stars and the planets
just flew from His hands.
He stocked sea with fish
and placed livestock on land.

What God made was awesome.
and funny, to boot.
Like aardvarks and hippos
and penguins in suits.

His work was amazing.
Creative. Unique.
Great forests of cedar,
oak, maple and teak.

Pink blossoms in springtime
and orange autumn leaves.
And even two people
called Adam and Eve.

* Read Genesis 1-2

A Man, A Woman and A Snake

The couple lived in Eden Park
where God would visit after dark.
And one such day the Lord explained
the facts of life. He made it plain.

"This garden's filled with vines and trees.
There's so much fruit. Enjoy them, please.

There're apples, apricots and cherries.
Grapefruit, pears and huckleberries.
Cumquats and papayas too.
Plums and lemons just for you.

I have only this one request.
Please listen closely. It's a test.
This is a chance for Me to tell
if you have ears that listen well.
If you have eyes that look to me
and hands that won't pick from *that* tree.
If you have feet that walk My way.
If you will trust Me and obey."

But a snake, a slippery serpent,
green and slimy, cold as ice,
slithered toward the man and woman
as they munched a ripe pear slice.

"Don't believe it. God's just kidding.
You can eat from every tree.
Go ahead and pick from *that* one.
It's delicious. Taste and see."

Oh, my goodness, they believed him
even though he was a snake.
That tree was the one they wanted.
Tiny bite but BIG MISTAKE.

*Read Genesis 3:1-24

Two Adams, Two Brides

In death-like sleep young Adam lay
so loneliness might pass away.
Then God reached down and pierced his side
and formed from Adam's rib a bride.

Eve drew her life from sinless man
and from her womb God's plan began.
It was her seed who grew by grace
to save old Adam's fallen race.

And as before, they pierced His side
the day the second Adam died.
It was a death that brought forth birth
in blood and water from His girth.

For from the Savior's bleeding side,
The Church was born --- His ransomed Bride.

* Read Romans 5:12-21

A Memorable Cruise

"Hey, Noah, get ready.
It's going to rain.
A gusher is coming.
So let Me be plain.

"I need you to build Me
a big honkin' boat.
Please follow the blueprints.
I want it to float."

So Noah got busy
and sawed up some boards.
He hammer and nailed them
and then asked the Lord,

"Is this what you're thinking?
This humongous ship
is why friends are laughing.
They're giving me lip."

"It's just like I wanted,"
the good Lord replied.
"Now go find some critters
to load up inside.

"A pair of Dalmatians,
a pair of brown slugs,
a pair of white stallions,
and two ladybugs.

"A couple of ostriches,
llamas and bats,
two elephants, reindeer,
hyenas and rats."

In no time the beasts
were all snug in their beds
and then without warning,
the sky overhead

got cloudy and darkish.
Drops fell with a thud.
It rained and it rained
till the drops made a flood.

But Noah was safe.
And his family was too.
And the boat that he'd built
was a real floating zoo.

When it finally quit raining
and the flood went away,
the cruise ship was emptied.
Whew! It smelled bad that day.

But, at least Noah's family
and the critters were spared.
The plans for an ark
proved that God really cared.

He hung out a rainbow
to promise His love.
So, remember you're special
when you see it above.

*Read Genesis 6-9.

Two Journeys to Moriah

To Mt. Moriah
Abraham leads his willing son.
Beneath the weight of the wood,
Isaac walks.
He stumbles.
He falls.
And as the father aims his dagger
at its intended target,
God calls from Heaven,
"It is finished!
The test is over!

Abraham, you passed.
You were willing.
All is well!"

Thirty centuries later
another willing Son
is led by His Father
to the same mountain.
Beneath the weight of wood,
Jesus walks.
He stumbles.
He falls.
Another pulls His weight for Him
to the place where soldiers will
spike his hands and feet
to two crossbeams of wood.
And as the willing
(and bleeding) Son waits to die,
He calls to Heaven,
"It is finished.
All's been paid for.
All is well!"

* Read Genesis 22:1-19

Down in the Pits

When you have ten older brothers,
you can feel a bit left out.
But Joseph had his father's love.
'Bout that there was no doubt.

Old Jacob gave the boy a coat
to prove his love for him.
Joe's brothers boiled with jealousy
and soon gave in to sin.

Pretending Joseph had been mauled,
they told their dad, "He's dead!"
When what they'd done was sell him
to a caravan instead.

In Pharaoh's land young Joe became
a prison warden's slave.
The Lord was with him and he thrived,
both handsome and behaved.

His boss's wife was smitten
by his strength and buffed physique.
She hoped her husband's attache
had morals that were weak.

But when young Joe rebuffed
her bold advances every night,
she falsely charged the slave with rape.
A cruel spurned woman's spite.

And once again Joe found himself
imprisoned in the pits.
But, he had faith in One who would
in time make sense of it.

*Read Genesis 39:1-23

A Dialogue Between Moses and God

When you face a Red Sea hurdle
and you're hemmed in from behind,
just recall how old man Moses
was about to lose his mind.

"God, I need you," Moses pleaded.
"Pharaoh's men are on my heels
and the Hebrew slaves here with me
know these obstacles are real."

And God answered, "Mo, no worry,
if you do what I have said.
I'm the Lord both of the Nile
and the Sea that's known as Red.

"I allow such opposition
so you'll realize your need.
That's the way your faith is nurtured.
You must learn to trust My lead."

"Thank you, Lord," old Moses whispered.
"Please forgive my fear and doubt.
All those plagues and burning bushes
are the proof You'll lead us out."

Just like that, the Red Sea parted.
All the Hebrews walked across.
But the soldiers of King Pharaoh
weren't as lucky. All were lost.

* Read Exodus 14:13-31

God's Happy (low-fat) Meals

When they left the land of Pharaoh
and headed to the east,
the Hebrews took their matzos dough
and made bread without yeast.

But soon their food had disappeared.
They heard their stomachs growl.
So God became like Jenny Craig,
providing low-fat fowl.

The quail flew near the ground so that
they easily were caught
before they would be barbecued
and eaten while still hot.

God's happy meals included more.
They weren't just for the birds.
A yogurt-white sweet breakfast food
appeared like whey and curds.

Each morning manna draped the ground,
like snow on Christmas Day.
They scooped it up before the sun
had melted it away.

Yes, God provided then as now.
He gave them daily bread.
And now as then we can give thanks
or grouse and gripe instead.

* Read Exodus 16

Barbecuing a Sacred Cow

You've heard about the fatted calf?
Let's kill this sacred cow.
The coals are on the barbecue.
The time to grill is now.

This beast's been treated like a god
entirely too long.
It's idol worship, is it not?
Like golden calves, it's wrong.

So let's have steaks and chops and ribs,
a brisket and a roast.
Some ground sirloin would be quite nice.
And tenderloin on toast.

Holy cow! Can't we agree?
This thing claims too much pull.
It's held us back from what God wants.
Quite sadly, that's no bull.

* Read Exodus 32

Giants in the Land

It's a desert that I'm dealing with
(this land of barren waste)
where I daily make a choice to stay "the call."
It's a wilderness, that's all.
The promised land of discipleship
is far from milk and honey anymore.

Sweet Jesus, there are giants in the land.
The hot breath of prowling lions singes my hope.
Power-hungry jackals stalk my joy.
Wolves, clothed like sheep, steal my trust.

The heat's always on in this land of shadows.
I'm tired. I'm thirsty. I'm tempted to quit.
It's about all I can take.

I'm aware of my enemies' presence.
But where are the green pastures and still waters?

Those succulent Egyptian melons
surely would taste good right now.
I could go for some garlic and leeks.
Lord, my resilience is weak.
And in the midst of this wilderness,
I ask that You find me.

* Read Numbers 11:1-15

Giant Grapes and More

Twelve spies sneaked in to check things out,
unsure of what they'd find.
What greeted them were giant grapes
just begging to be wine.

The pomegranates and the figs
were juicy, plump and ripe.
The Land was all God had described.
Still, all but two spies griped.

"The grapes are bigger than we've seen
That's absolutely true.
But that's not all that's really big.
The land boasts giants too.

"In spite of all that awesome fruit,
we'd be in quite a jam
to try and claim what God insists
is our long-promised land."

And so the ten convinced the rest
they'd best not move ahead.
Just Josh and Caleb trusted God.
The others tasted dread.

* Read Numbers 13

Rock Pile

There's a rock pile near a river
that was heaped up long ago.
It's an altar of remembrance
so that all who see will know

what God did to help His people.
How He led them by His hand.
How He moved both earth and heaven
so they'd reach the Promised Land.

It was built so they'd remember
how the Jordan River halved,
when the Lord piled up the water
to create a safe, dry path.

When their kids and grandkids saw it,
they were overheard to ask,
"What's the point of all these boulders
that for centuries still last?"

"They are what is called an altar.
Ebenezer. Visual aid.
It's a tangible reminder
how God saved us when we prayed."

* Read Joshua 4

Standing Up to Goliath

That pagan giant cursed and swore,
blaspheming Israel's God.
And standing almost ten feet tall,
Goliath looked quite odd.

King Saul's poor army hid in fear,
unsure of what to do.
And though they had good cause for faith,
they didn't trust. Would you?

Would you be willing to stand up
like teenage David did?
He dared to trust the living God,
although he was a kid.

The way the giant dragged God's name
in that Philistine dirt
made David mad. It wasn't right.
His shepherd's heart felt hurt.

A slingshot and just one smooth stone
was all young David needed.
In one fell swoop Goliath died.
The shepherd boy succeeded.

But that isn't all…

Goliaths with new names still taunt.
They mock the Lord we serve.
These giants laugh at what God says
and rob us of our nerve.

They put down we, who follow Christ,
and claim that we're extreme.
And just like David, we react.
God-slamming is obscene.

These giant critics pack much weight.
Their values dwarf us all.
What can we do to counter them?
They stand Goliath-tall.

But we can't be preoccupied
with reasons why we can't.
God uses those who (when compared
to giants) look like ants.

* Read 1 Samuel 17

The Gospel According to Mephibosheth

King Saul had a grandson with quite a long name.
Mephibosheth's plight caused the boy endless shame.

His legs badly crippled meant he couldn't walk.
He crawled like a beggar, embarrassed to talk.

Young Bo dreamed of living his life off the ground,
released from the prison that held the boy bound.

He hoped and he waited. Mephibosheth prayed.
And one day the cost of Bo's freedom was paid.

A shepherd named David became Israel's king,
and hearing of Bo gave the boy cause to sing.

He welcomed young Bo with his weak twisted legs.
"You'll sit at my table. No more will you beg.

"As long as you live you'll be part of my clan.
You'll sit up with dignity. That is God's plan."

* Read 2 Samuel 4:1-4; 9:1-13

King David's Other Giant

When kings were s'pose to go to war,
King David stayed at home.
And late one night he couldn't sleep,
so took a walk alone.

From where he stood, he saw a sight
from which he should have turned.
But David chose to fantasize
and fueled a lust that burned.

Another war of sorts raged on.
How would the king respond?
Would he defeat the enemy,
as darkness caved to dawn?

He was no stranger to a fight.
He'd killed the Philistine.
He'd run from Saul, yet took his crown.
At wars, he wasn't green.

And yet...

Temptation won this tug of war.
Goliath's killer lost.

An inner giant slew the king.
He didn't count the cost.

And so it is with greedy lust.
It longs to claim the throne.
When left unchecked, it rules the heart
and wrecks a leader's home.

The moral? Always be on guard.
Don't think that you're exempt.
When you make claims of being strong,
then Satan's bound to tempt.

* Read 2 Samuel 11

Bathsheba's Psalm

I feel dirty, my Lord,
despised and impure.
Did Your eyes not see
the eyes of my king
robbing me of my privacy?
Lost in lonely, anxious thoughts,
I bathed in silence,
unaware of being watched.
My carefree heart was heavy.
My perfumed bed empty.
My beloved Uriah far away at war.
And then the unthinkable...

From the castle came the guardsmen,
and, as if I were a common whore,
I was led to the royal bed.
He searched me, O God.

He "knew" me.
I was the subject of David's
unquenchable carnal knowledge.
Before the velvet black dissolved
into the bluish sky of dawn,
how I wanted to die, my Lord.

Kidnapped by lust, a hostage of desire,
I was reduced to a pile of kindling
enveloped by passion's fire.
In the span of a few hours,
a contented, happy bride,
a carefree daughter of the day,
became an unwilling woman of the night.
And if that weren't enough,
my plight of injustice grew worse.

In my violated womb, a child.
On the battlefield, a lifeless husband.
On my infant's bed, a baby dead.
And in my shattered heart, shards of grief
and the hope that (in time) You'll heal me.

* Read Psalm 27

Naomi's Redemption

My husband, our two boys and I
moved far from Bethlehem.
We settled east of Jordan banks
in what's called Moab land.

I missed my friends and family.
I had good cause to cry.

That's what I thought, until (good Lord)
my husband up and died.

I missed him so. We were best friends.
I tried to move ahead.
And just when things were going well,
my married sons fell dead.

"Now what to do?" I asked the Lord.
"I can't go on alone."
It seemed to me I heard him say,
"Naomi, move back home!"

And as I packed, my dead son's wife
surprised me as she said,
"Where you now go, I want to too.
That's how I'm feeling led."

So we returned (the two of us)
to little Bethlehem,
where God would soon provide for Ruth
a very wealthy man.

But that's not all God would provide
within that tiny town.
To Boaz's bride (though Gentile born)
the Lord would give renown.

You may not know Ruth's great-grandson
would play the harp and sing.
He was the slingshot shepherd boy
who grew up to be king.

* Read Ruth 1-4

The Wise Fool

King Solomon was quite a man,
the wisest yet to live.
But due to his divided heart,
his brain became a sieve.

He failed to heed the truth he knew,
ignoring what God said.
His pagan wives and foreign gods
took precedence instead.

The once-wise king became a fool,
as any fool can see.
In spite of wealth, he died quite poor
in moral bankruptcy.

* Read 1 Kings 11:1-13

Confessions of a Modern-day Job

When you lose your job, you feel like Job.
It seems you've lost it all.
The world looks gray and colorless
and tastes like bitter gall.

You seek the Lord, but He won't speak.
You lose your will to pray.
And when your "good" friends try to help,
you wish they'd go away.

Quite insecure, you doubt your worth.
You try in vain to hope.
You feel alone. You feel afraid
(without the means to cope).

It's so unfair to be let go.
You gave your heart and soul.
While others loafed, you sacrificed
to reach your boss's goal.

Your sleep declines. Your bills add up.
Resentment stays the same.
You don't know what or who to call.
You don't know where to aim.

No business card. No payroll check.
You have no place to go.
Without a job in our culture,
you are a big "zero".

And still, I know deep in my heart
God thinks that I'm a "10".
My worth to Him does not consist
in what I do (or when).

He's gifted me and knows my skills
and loves me as I am.
And so, from Job, I'll take my cues
and trust God's unseen plan.

* Read Job 19

Shepherd of Goodness (Psalm 23)

Shepherd of Goodness, Your mercy has found us
here in green pastures where Your kingdom grows.
Cleansed by the waters of new birth, we offer
praise to Your goodness that saves and restores.

Shepherd of Goodness, Your presence is with us
when death's cold shadows seem too much to bear.
Those who You call to provide for our comfort,
point to Your goodness through preaching and prayer.

Shepherd of Goodness, Your table invites us.
Bread for our hunger, a cup of new wine.
Nourished by grace we can face opposition,
led by Your goodness and sovereign design.

Shepherd of Goodness, on this blest occasion,
we are reminded that You're in control.
Weaving our past with the days yet before us,
You're our Good Shepherd. Your love we extol.

* Read Psalm 23

The Lord is My Caddy

A golfer looks at Psalm 23.

Because the Lord is my Caddy,
I have everything that I need.
When my lies are deep down in green pastures,
or when I face hazards disguised as still waters,
He guides me through each shot with confidence.
When I lose my footing,
He restores my soles with new spikes.

Even though I walk through tree-lined shadows
only to find my ball buried in a sand trap
(reminiscent of Death Valley),
I'm not inclined to worry.
My Caddy hands me my wedge
(along with His rod and His staff)

and comforts me with,
"Keep your eye on the ball, don't over swing
and all will be okay!"

When I finally reach the table-like green
and it seems my opponent's sure to take the lead,
my Caddy goes before me, stepping off my putt.
He prepares me for the way it will break.
When I take time to listen to His voice
and follow His advice,
the cup overflows with that priceless sound
of a ball that has finally found its home.

For goodness' sake, such mercy.
When I shank and hook
(and at times slice) my ball astray,
my Caddy is right beside me, reminding me
that the eighteenth hole is not that far away.

* Read Psalm 23

Psalm 121 in Rhyme

Everywhere I look around me,
there are peaks too high to climb.
I am dwarfed by difficulties.
I'm o'ershadowed most the time.

How can I ascend these mountains?
Are there ways to tunnel through?
Obstacles are claustrophobic.
Panicking is nothing new.

When I'm prone to think it's over
and there's nothing to be done,
in my heart I hear a whisper
telling me to fear no one.

It's the voice of Him who loves me.
He contends I need not fret.
When He feels I'm in real danger,
He will act and not forget.

God is always looking at me.
From His vantage point He sees
all the details I am blind to.
That's why He says, "Trust Me please!"

Though I think I have to worry
as if fretting pays the freight,
God my maker dwarfs the mountains
of those hills I fear and hate.

* Read Psalm 121

A Proverbs 31 Mother

A Christ-like mother's hard to find.
Someone whose character is kind.
A woman who spends time in prayer,
before the day begins.

A Christ-like mother runs her home,
just like a queen upon her throne.
She finds out what her subjects need
and then provides for them.

BIBLE DAYS

A Christ-like mother finds the time
to plug the piggy bank with dimes
from what she makes for what she does
outside the home and in.

A Christ-like mother plans ahead.
She shops for milk, ground beef and bread.
But all the while, she asks the Lord
to guide the way she spends.

A Christ-like mother never sleeps
until she comforts kids who weep
because of broken toys and hearts.
In her, they see God's love.

A Christ-like mother is the key
to maximize a family
so it becomes all that it can,
providing roots and wings.

A Christ-like mother sets the stage
for fueling joy and calming rage.
Her attitude infects the home
with germs most sure to spread.

A Christ-like mother and a wife
won't let her home be filled with strife.
She takes the lead to call a truce
and sort through all the facts.

A Christ-like mother loves her man
the way the Source of marriage planned.
She seeks to serve his many needs
while letting him meet hers.

A Christ-like mother may grow old
with silver hair and teeth of gold.
But wrinkles only frame a face
that boasts a timeless smile.

A Christ-like mother leaves behind
what progeny are sure to find...
The footprints of a faithful life
that sought God's kingdom first.

* Read Proverbs 31:10-31

A Life and Legacy Recalled

A godly Hebrew, buffed and bright
in far off Babylon,
was dreaming of Jerusalem,
the place from which he'd come.

Young Belteshazzar faced the west
and prayed three times a day.
Dismayed by what his God allowed
and where he'd likely stay.

But Daniel and his kosher friends
did not stoop to complain.
They stood their ground (and knelt in praise),
while calling on God's name.

They didn't do what most folk did.
They swam against the tide.
Instead of eating royal fare,
they let God be their guide.

A fiery furnace proved their faith
was pure as precious gold.
A den of lions tested Dan
and found him brave and bold.

Integrity. That's what Dan had.
And cryptic visions too.
The prophecies that he wrote down
brought end times into view.

He spoke about the Son of Man
and how He would prevail
with all who finally realize
that godless efforts fail.

O, Danny Boy, I love your book.
It's filled with mystery.
From Babylon to where I live,
your life and words reach me.

* Read Daniel 1-3

Lessons from Jonah

When God said, "Go to Nineveh!"
Joe sighed a loud "Oy Vay!"
But that was not the worst of it.
He ran the other way.

Joe then booked passage on a cruise
to drown God's still small voice.
But it was he who nearly drowned.
The captain had no choice.

When winds and waves came bearing down
that made the vessel tip,
this minor prophet owned the blame.
That's when Jonah jumped ship.

But deep beneath the churning tide,
God placed a special fish,
who only had an appetite
for one disgusting dish.

The fish threw up and Joe flew out.
He landed on a beach.
And just like that, God changed the heart
of one He'd called to preach.

The lesson here is fairly plain.
When God calls us to go,
we'll save ourselves a lot of grief
if we don't run like Joe.

* Read Jonah 1-4

My Favorite Gospel Quartet

There's a gospel quartet
I have followed for years.
Their lyrics have prompted
reflection and tears.

Four men who know Jesus,
who belt out good news.
Whose repertoire features
God's unchanging truths.

Four guys with a message
who greet me each dawn.
There's Matthew and Mark.
Then there's Luke and then John.

Such four distinct voices
have great harmony.
My favorite quartet
is a blessing to me.

* Read Matthew 1, Mark 1, Luke 1 and John 1

A Leper No Longer

A Shepherd to a leper said,
"Your skin is dead no longer!
The rotting flesh and lifeless nerves
(that defined you far too long) are gone.
They have camouflaged
your true identity long enough.
What was diseased is healthy once again.
Precious lamb, I have healed you.
Let me carry you.
Nuzzle your cold, wet, trembling nose
in the crook of my strong, unwavering arm.
No harm will befall you.
I have called you by name,
a name that others have forgotten
(if they knew at all).
A name that invites your dignity and worth
to stand up and take a bow
unashamed."

* Read Matthew 8:1-4

My Friend Matthew

My friend Matthew's well worth knowing.
Like my neighbors, he's a Jew.
He's a taxman by profession,
but, in some ways, he's like you.

He met Jesus, was converted,
changed careers which means, I'd guess,
that he lost his perks and pension
when he left the IRS.

Matt became a Christian writer
and no doubt you've read his book.
If you haven't, well, you ought to.
It's non-fiction with a hook.

It recounts the life of Jesus
from a Jewish point of view.
Matt's accountant-driven detail
makes good reading. Plus it's true.

It's the longest of the gospels.
It's the first one of the four.
It contains that famous sermon,
plus the magi and the star.

It is worthy of much study.
Matthew's book can change your life.
It's a source of inspiration
with a sharp edge like a knife.

* Read Matthew 9:9-13
** *I wrote this especially for the Community Bible Study class
that meets at our church on Mercer Island.*

Jesus' Bar Mitzvah

When making their trip back to Nazareth one day,
the mother of Jesus was noted to say,
"He's missing. Where is he? My son isn't here."
The strain in her voice signaled unvarnished fear.

The panic persisted. All stones were unturned.
The air was electric with caution well-earned.
And then someone shouted, "The boy has been found.
He's there in the Temple. He's on holy ground."

They rushed to the elders and there in their midst
was a confident, talkative twelve-year-old kid.
"Young man!" Mary chided.
"You've caused us much grief."
"But mother!" he answered. "You've really no beef."

"It shouldn't surprise you that I would be here.
My Father's agenda demands it. That's clear.
This is my bar mitzvah. Today I'm a man.
Please cut me some slack as I live out God's plan."

* Read Luke 2:14-52

Becoming More Like Mary

While her sister stirred the stew,
Mary knew what she must do.
And with rapt attention
focused on the Lord she dearly loved.

Hanging on His every word,
Mary listened undisturbed
by the sound of clanking dishes
just beyond the living room.

Sitting at the Savior's feet,
Mary had no need to eat.
She was nourished by sweet moments
that were honey to her soul.

Having Jesus in her home
was a feast she'd never known.
She had learned to leave the kitchen
and escape the day's demands.

And though we cannot see Him there,
utilize an empty chair
to remind yourself that everyday
the Lord wants time with you.

* Read Luke 10:38-42

The Rich Fool

He had a bumper crop that year
on his enormous farm.
"Good God, I'm rich!" the farmer crowed.
"I need a bigger barn!"

A richer man there never was.
Quite wealthy, but unwise.
He failed to glean from Wisdom's store.
"Who reaps much, also dies."

* Read Luke 12:13-21

Walls Fall Down

Jesus drew near to Jericho,
a city of palm trees where long before
Joshua watched city walls fall.
But on this day, walls of another kind fell.
Unseen walls that surround the human heart
keeping out the very thing you need the most.

Laying his pride aside, a friend of few
(barely five feet two in height) climbed a tree.
Zacchaeus wanted to see for himself
if what others were saying was true.
Something about a certain Someone
who accepted people just as they were.
This Someone in question
didn't care about labels
like Gentile, Samaritan or Jew.
Being a tax collector,
Zach had been labeled long enough.
He longed to be loved, forgiven and free.
And so he climbed a sycamore tree
to watch as this Someone walked by.

The tree he chose was different
from all the others in town.
And so was this Teacher who invited him down
to spend the day together.
As the little man fell to his knees,
the walls of pride and greed
(that had barricaded his heart for years) crumbled.
No need for Joshua's trumpets this time.

And before the day was over, an unlikely disciple
(no longer needing a tree) stood tall.

* Read Luke 19:1-10

The Gospel According to You

A man known as John wrote a Gospel
so that we might believe in God's Son.
It is based on the things that he witnessed
in the life of One second to none.

It's a Gospel that's really poetic.
It has all kinds of figures of speech.
As you read what he wrote, it's like being
by John's side as he heard Jesus teach.

It's a Gospel that's unlike the others.
It is simple, yet deeply profound.
There are layers of truth in each chapter
that through study are peeled back and found.

It's a Gospel with transforming power.
As you prayerfully ponder each page,
may the Spirit who prompted its writing
grant you wisdom befitting a sage.

In the end may the Word become flesh-like,
as you incarnate Christ in your walk.
May the truths in this book be reflected
in your actions, not simply in talk.

May the Gospel of John spark fresh insights
that remind you that Scripture is true.
May the outcome of what John has written
be the Gospel according to you.

* Read John 1:1-14

Water into You-Know-What

The bride and groom had broken glass.
The dancing had begun.
The friends and family cut the rug.
They all were having fun.

That is until the caterer
announced embarrassedly,
"The wine's run out. The merlot's gone.
There's also no Chablis."

A laughingstock, that's what I'll be
if word of this gets out.
My reputation's sure to tank.
About that there's no doubt.

When Mary heard, she told her son
about the beverage glitch.
The Savior didn't skip a beat,
for Him there was no hitch.

"Just fill some jars with H20,"
The Lord was heard to say.
"Then pour it out and serve it up.
You'll like this vin rose."

And with the first sip someone said,
"Now where'd you find this cask?"
Unlike most weddings I've been to,
you've saved the best till last."

Read John 2:1-11

A Night of Thirst

At Jacob's well,
a woman sat to rest a spell
and drink from a spring
of cool, refreshing water.

Her jug was heavy.
So was her heart.
So many hurts
and disappointed hopes.

How could she make it?
How could she cope?
How could she stumble on?

Little did she realize
that right before her weary eyes,
her night of thirst and gnawing fear
was giving way to dawn.

* Read John 4:1-42

A Little Boy and His Lunch

When that young kid gave up his lunch,
did those disciples have a hunch
of how five loaves and two small fish
would feed a multitude?

I rather think they thought it bunk.
There's just no way they could have thunk
that tuna sandwich fixins would
accomplish such a feat.

I'm pretty certain Jesus beamed
at childlike faith he'd never seen,
as one so short showed faith that stood
much taller than his years.

* Read John 6:1-15

Praying in the Spirit

At times in prayer I lack for words
and utter sounds some think absurd.
I break into an unknown tongue
my Father understands.

The Spirit deep within me sighs
with moanings God can recognize.
My Comforter discerns my thoughts
and translates what I need.

My language is a gift from God.
It's nothing strange. It's hardly odd.
It is a means by which my prayer
can flow most naturally.

* Read Romans 8:26-27 and I Corinthians 14:1-5

In the Fullness of Time

Full of grace,
full of fear,
full of child nearly born,
barely able to balance herself
on a donkey's bumpy back,

Mary, with her man,
makes her way to Bethlehem.
Full of people responding to Caesar's census,
this little town lies strangely still,
except for the screams of this child-with-child
(strangely still a virgin) who labors long and hard
full of God… pushing Him into the world.
As Mary's screams give way to her baby's borning cry,
she cradles her Creator to her breast, full of awe.
And then she falls asleep,
full of peace.
Redemption's time had fully come at last!

* Read Galatians 3:26-4:7

A Trophy of God's Grace
Poetic reflections on First Peter

When the heat is on and you wonder
if you can really take the fire,
please remember what God promised
in His Word.

The flame is your friend.
In the end, it won't melt you.
The scorching torch of suffering
has a limit to its burn.
It has a holy purpose.

You see, when the Father
tries your faith by fire,
His desire isn't just to test your mettle.
He doesn't want you to settle
for anything less than the best

He has for you.
And to get to that point, there is dross
that must be burned away.

In His eyes, you're like precious metal,
a treasure of beauty,
worthy of the process that it takes to purify.
He wants to bring you to the place where
you're a trophy of His grace.

So let the flame achieve its goal.
When you've stood the test (still standing),
those nearby will be amazed.

* Read 1 Peter 1:3-12

A One-Volume Library

There is more to the Bible
than first meets the eye.

It's a doctrinal diary,
a history book,
a collection of letters
(each one with a hook).

It's a hymnal of lyrics,
a journal of pain,
a digest of proverbs
(to read time and again).

It's a handbook of wisdom,
a volume of prayer.
It's the story of Jesus
that's bound to be shared.

* Read Hebrews 4:12-13

Revelation Revealed

An island. A vision.
A dragon. A beast.
A lamb on a throne
and a great wedding feast.

It's called Revelation.
It seems like Sci-Fi.
A bottomless pit
and a crystal-sea sky.

A book meant for travelers,
who love a great ride.
So much is confusing,
but stay at it and try.

Attack Revelation.
Let your pastor help guide.
He'll point out the love
Jesus has for His Bride.

* Read Revelation 1:4-20

In Praise of the Coming King

In the story of the ages,
the King of Kings and Lord of Lords
gallops toward the end of time
with majesty and glory.

No longer saddled on a borrowed burro,
He speeds His way on a snow-white steed.
Freed from Death's dark doorless prison,
He rides from the pages of old John's vision
across the miles of centuries
into our harrowed lives.

Ride on, victorious Jesus.
Ride on with keys in hand.
Dead-bolt our fears.
Unlock our minds
so we can understand
Your triumphant presence,
Your never-failing strength,
and the edicts of Your sovereign rule
that know no breadth nor length.

Hallelujah! Maranatha!
Ride on, King Jesus, ride!
Reclaim Your world. Receive our praise.
Revive Your slumbering Bride.

* Read Revelation 19:11-16

Maranatha

Caught in the traffic of daily distresses,
trapped in routines that have lost their appeal,
weary of holding to dreams that allude us,
maranatha, Lord Jesus, we await your return.

Jaded by broken commitments and losses,
reeling from setbacks that rob our reserves,
fearing the words of a doctor's announcement,
maranatha, Lord Jesus, we await your return.

Troubled by cultural trends that are godless,
doubting decisions the courts claim as fair,
haunted by laughter that mocks human kindness
maranatha, Lord Jesus, we await your return.

Longing for what you intended in Eden,
hoping for meaning beyond what we see,
looking for ultimate justice and mercy,
maranatha, Lord Jesus, we await your return.

* Read Revelation 22:7-21

Route 66

There's a trip that's well worth taking.
It's been called Route 66.
It's a highway from a garden
to a street of golden bricks.

It's an interstate connecting
what God did in ancient days
to what still awaits in Heaven,
marked by songs of endless praise.

BIBLE DAYS

I love traveling this roadway
as I read God's Holy Word.
Every twist and turn reminds me
I have cause to be assured.

There are sixty-six great reasons
you should journey through His Book.
It's a trek that's best made slowly,
with eyes open so to look

at the landscape of redemption
and the valleys of despair.
Don't forget the mountain summits
where God demonstrates He's there.

Note the badlands of wrong choices
and the harvest fields of grace.
As you travel through the Scriptures,
find yourself in every place.

** I wrote this poem for my congregation as we setoff on an
adventure we called "Route 66." During that year we read
through all sixty-six books of the Bible. Each Sunday my
sermon was based on our weekly readings.*

35739117R00162

Made in the USA
Charleston, SC
18 November 2014